CW00546653

"THE FREER I GET, THE HIGHER I GO.
THE HIGHER I GO, THE MORE I SEE.
THE MORE I SEE, THE LESS I KNOW.
THE LESS I KNOW, THE MORE I'M FREE."

– RAM DASS

A COOKBOOK, HANDMADE FOR THE
MIND, BODY AND SOUL.

by Matthew & Rebecca Teague

DISCLAIMER

THE BASIC PREMISE OF THIS BOOK IS TO HELP BRING YOU INTO BALANCE USING GOOD FOOD AND DRINK.

THROUGH CREATING AND CONSUMING THE RECIPES IN THIS BOOK, YOU TAKE FULL RESPONSIBILITY FOR THE HEALTH OF YOURSELF AND ANYONE ELSE CONSUMING THEM.

WE DO NOT CLAIM TO CURE ANY DISEASE OR ILLNESS USING THE METHODS PROVIDED IN THIS BOOK, AND SO WE TAKE NO RESPONSIBILITY FOR ANY OUTCOME OF ADVERSE HEALTH.

THE INFORMATION IN THIS BOOK IS NOT INTENDED AS A REPLACEMENT FOR ANY CONVENTIONAL MEDICINE YOU MAY BE TAKING - IT IS MERELY A SUPPLEMENT TO A HEALTHY LIFESTYLE.

WE RECOMMEND THAT YOU CONSULT A MEDICAL PRACTITIONER BEFORE USING THIS BOOK IF YOU SUFFER FROM ANY SERIOUS MEDICAL CONDITIONS.

ABOVE ALL, HONOUR YOUR INTUITION - IT GOT YOU THIS FAR!

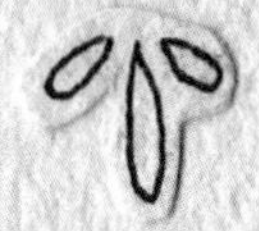

DEDICATIONS

TO OUR DEAR FAMILY, WHO TAUGHT US THE VALUE OF GOOD FOOD, AND EVEN BETTER COMPANY.

AND SPECIAL THANKS TO OUR PARENTS, WHO PROVIDED US THE SPACE TO CREATE.

WE LOVE YOU AND ARE FOREVER GRATEFUL FOR YOUR PATIENCE.

ONLY ONE KITCHEN WAS HARMED IN THE MAKING OF THIS COOKBOOK.

contents
LOVE THE FOOD THAT EVENTUALLY BECOMES YOU.

Introduction

recipes

FOREWORD

WELL, WHAT AN INSPIRING, BEAUTIFUL AND TIMELY BOOK THE TEAGUES HAVE CREATED.

FULL OF INSIGHTS, PRACTICAL KNOWLEDGE AND WISDOM.
BEAUTIFULLY CRAFTED AND SYNERGISTICALLY ASSEMBLED WITH BECS' UNIQUE STYLE OF ART AND MATT'S KEEN LENS. THIS LABOUR OF LOVE WAS SYMBIOTICALLY BIRTHED FROM THEIR PASSION FOR PLANT-BASED NUTRITION AND CONSCIOUS LIVITY.

DIET CHANGE NOT CLIMATE CHANGE HAS BECOME THE CLARION CALL OF OUR GENERATION AND THIS BOOK EMPOWERS SUCH WISDOM THROUGH WELL TESTED RECIPES THAT ARE EASY TO FOLLOW, YIELDING GREAT FLAVOURS AND NUTRITION.

AS HUMANITY RAPIDLY MOVES TOWARDS SUSTAINABLE ORGANIC FARMING PRACTICES TO FEED ITSELF WITHOUT DEVOURING THE PLANET, GEMS LIKE BABA'S BITES WILL PLAY AN IMPORTANT ROLE IN SPREADING THE KNOWLEDGE AND LOVE NEEDED TO MAKE THE DIFFERENCE.

OPEN THIS BOOK AND TREAD GENTLY ON MOTHER EARTH WHILST FEEDING YOUR BODY, MIND AND HEART.

ALL IS ONE & ONE IS ALL.

BOBSY
FOUNDER OF MANA! H.K.
MAY 25TH 2021

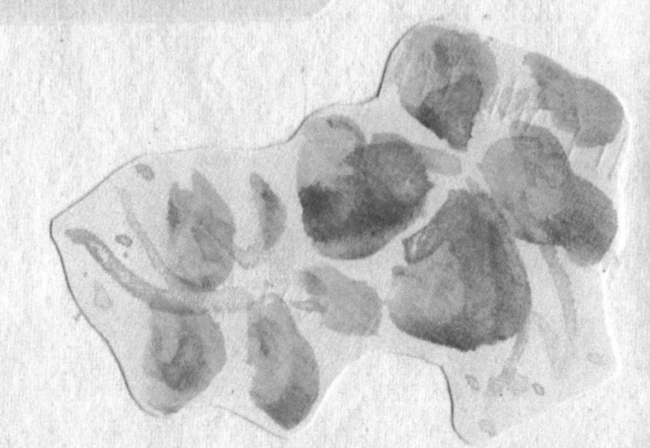

WHO IS THIS BOOK FOR?

THIS BOOK IS PERFECT FOR...

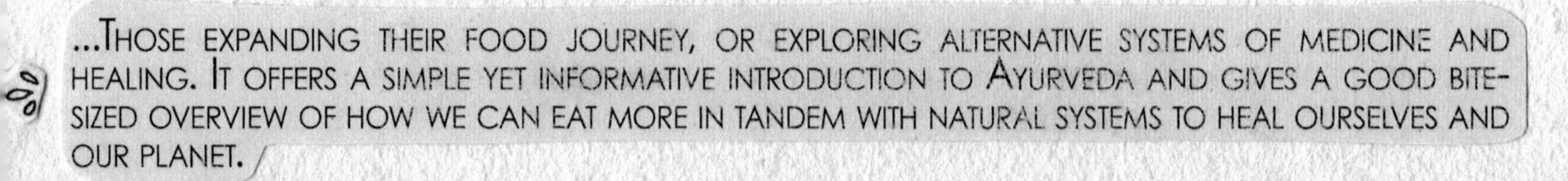

...THOSE EXPANDING THEIR FOOD JOURNEY, OR EXPLORING ALTERNATIVE SYSTEMS OF MEDICINE AND HEALING. IT OFFERS A SIMPLE YET INFORMATIVE INTRODUCTION TO AYURVEDA AND GIVES A GOOD BITE-SIZED OVERVIEW OF HOW WE CAN EAT MORE IN TANDEM WITH NATURAL SYSTEMS TO HEAL OURSELVES AND OUR PLANET.

...THOSE WANTING TO BE MORE CONSCIOUS OF THE IMPACT THAT THEIR DIET IS HAVING ON OUR PLANET. THIS BOOK, WITH IT'S SEASONAL APPROACH TO FOOD, NATURALLY SIMPLIFIES OUR FOOD CHOICES AND LESSENS OUR ENVIRONMENTAL IMPACT.

...THOSE WHO HAVE ADOPTED A PLANT-BASED DIET YET FIND THEMSELVES RELYING ON PROCESSED, UNNATURAL FOODS AND STRANGE MEAT ALTERNATIVES. THIS BOOK WILL PROVIDE AN ACCESSIBLE INSIGHT INTO A WHOLE-FOODS APPROACH TO LIVING WITHOUT MEAT AND DAIRY.

WE'VE MADE THIS BOOK FOR ANYONE AND EVERYONE WHO WOULD WANT TO ADD A LITTLE MORE CONSCIOUSNESS TO THEIR FOOD CHOICES. WE BELIEVE THAT THE WISDOM OFFERED HERE CAN HELP ON THE ROAD TO UNDERSTANDING WHAT WE PUT IN OUR BODIES, HOW TO EAT MORE NATURALLY AND LESSEN OUR TOXIC BURDENS.

WE RECOMMEND THIS BOOK TO BE USED AS A SUPPLEMENT TO AN ALREADY HEALTHY AND BALANCED DIET.

BABA' S BITES IS A COOKBOOK CREATED BY US,
TWO SIBLINGS ON A JOURNEY OF DISCOVERING WELLNESS AND HEALING THROUGH FOOD AND AYURVEDA.

TOGETHER, WE HAVE BOTH COME TO KNOW THE IMPORTANCE OF RIGHT EATING AS A CORE FOUNDATION FOR HUMAN AND PLANETARY HEALTH. THE RIGHT SOIL MAKES HEALTHY FOOD, WHICH FEEDS A HEALTHY BALANCED BODY. THEN, THIS BODY CAN CREATE A STRONG FOUNDATION FOR THE MIND AND SOUL TO FLOURISH, AND IN TURN A HEALTHY PLANET BLOSSOMS.

IT' S CLEAR THAT MODERN AGRICULTURAL PRACTICES HAVE LED TO A DEPLETION OF BASIC AND ESSENTIAL NUTRIENTS IN THE TOPSOIL OF OUR EARTH. IT IS NO COINCIDENCE THAT OUR BODIES MAY BE FEELING A LACK OF VITALITY, WITH MANY PEOPLE NOW SEARCHING FOR MORE NATURAL AND ORGANIC WAYS TO IMPROVE THEIR PHYSICAL, MENTAL AND SPIRITUAL WELL-BEING.

THE NEEDS FOR A VARIED AND BALANCED DIET, INCREASED EDUCATION AND AWARENESS, AND PLANETARY PROTECTION COME HAND-IN-HAND. THIS HOLISTIC LENS ON LIFE, SUPPORTED BY ANCIENT MYSTICAL WISDOM OF NATURE AND BALANCE, CAN REKINDLE THE BELIEF THAT OUR EARTH ALREADY HOLDS EVERYTHING WE NEED TO HEAL, AND BE HEALED IN RETURN.

THIS BOOK AIMS TO TACKLE OUR OWN LITTLE PORTION OF THE BIGGER PICTURE, WITH A HOPE OF GIVING PEOPLE A STRONGER UNDERSTANDING OF HOW FOOD CAN BE USED AS MEDICINE
- TO BRING HUMANS BACK INTO HARMONY WITH NATURE THROUGH SIMPLY EATING WELL.

BEYOND 'BABA' S BITES', MATTHEW AND REBECCA RUN THEIR 'BABA' S' PLATFORM, WHICH OFFERS INTEGRATIVE THERAPY MODALITIES SUCH AS AYURVEDIC CONSULTANCY, YOGA, BREATHWORK, ENERGY WORK, WORKSHOPS, EVENTS AND MORE.

REBECCA

With a passion to make a sweet little mark on the world Rebecca is the younger half of the sibling duo, honorary sous-chef and the paintbrush behind our illustrations and creations.

Away from the drawing board, Rebecca practices as a certified Yoga and Ayurveda Wellness Consultant, Energy Work Practitioner, Occupational Therapist and Yoga Teacher, while currently furthering her training to become a Psychotherapist in London, UK.

Over the past 10 years, Rebecca has personally used Ayurvedic principles and other alternative healing modalities to reverse a number of chronic imbalances within her hormonal, emotional and gut health.

Alongside her brother, Baba's Bites is a creation of holding hands in the power of expression, community and a hope to continue to share the wisdom of these practices, with each person's individuality at heart.

She wishes you to feel held in your endeavours and empowered to create positive change worldwide through the creations in this book.

MATTHEW

BOTH THE HANDS BEHIND THE FOOD AND CAMERA SHUTTER, MATTHEW' S CREATIVITY AND LOVE COME INTUITIVELY IN CONSCIOUSLY COMBINING INGREDIENTS. HE BELIEVES THAT ONE' S CONNECTION TO FOOD AND ITS ORIGINS NATURALLY CONNECT THEM TO THEIR ROOTS - SYMBOLICALLY AND LITERALLY.

HIS WELL-ROUNDED AND HOLISTIC SCOPE ON THE PLANETARY AND HUMAN DILEMMAS THAT WE FACE HAS BEEN INSPIRED BY HIS STUDIES OF HUMAN GEOGRAPHY, FOOD SYSTEMS AND PERMACULTURE, ALONGSIDE A DEEPENING PASSION IN EASTERN APPROACHES OF AYURVEDA AND ENERGETICS. HE IS MOVED TO UNDERSTAND HOW WE CAN FUSE THE WISDOM OF THESE SCHOOLS TO CREATE SOLUTIONS FOR OUR INNER AND OUTER BIOMES.

NOW A CERTIFIED AYURVRDIC LIFESTYLE CONSULTANT AND BREATHWORK PRACTICIONER, MATTHEW CURRENTLY COOKS WHOLESOME AND HEALING FOODS WHILE TRAVELLING TO EVENTS AND RETREATS WORLDWIDE. HE DREAMS TO SHARE HIS WISDOM AND OFFERINGS AT HIS OWN RESTAURANT ONE DAY.

HE SEES STRENGTH IN COMBINING HIS VISION WITH HIS SISTER' S, WHO IS ON A REMARKABLY SIMILAR TRAJECTORY. HENCE, BABA' S WAS BORN.

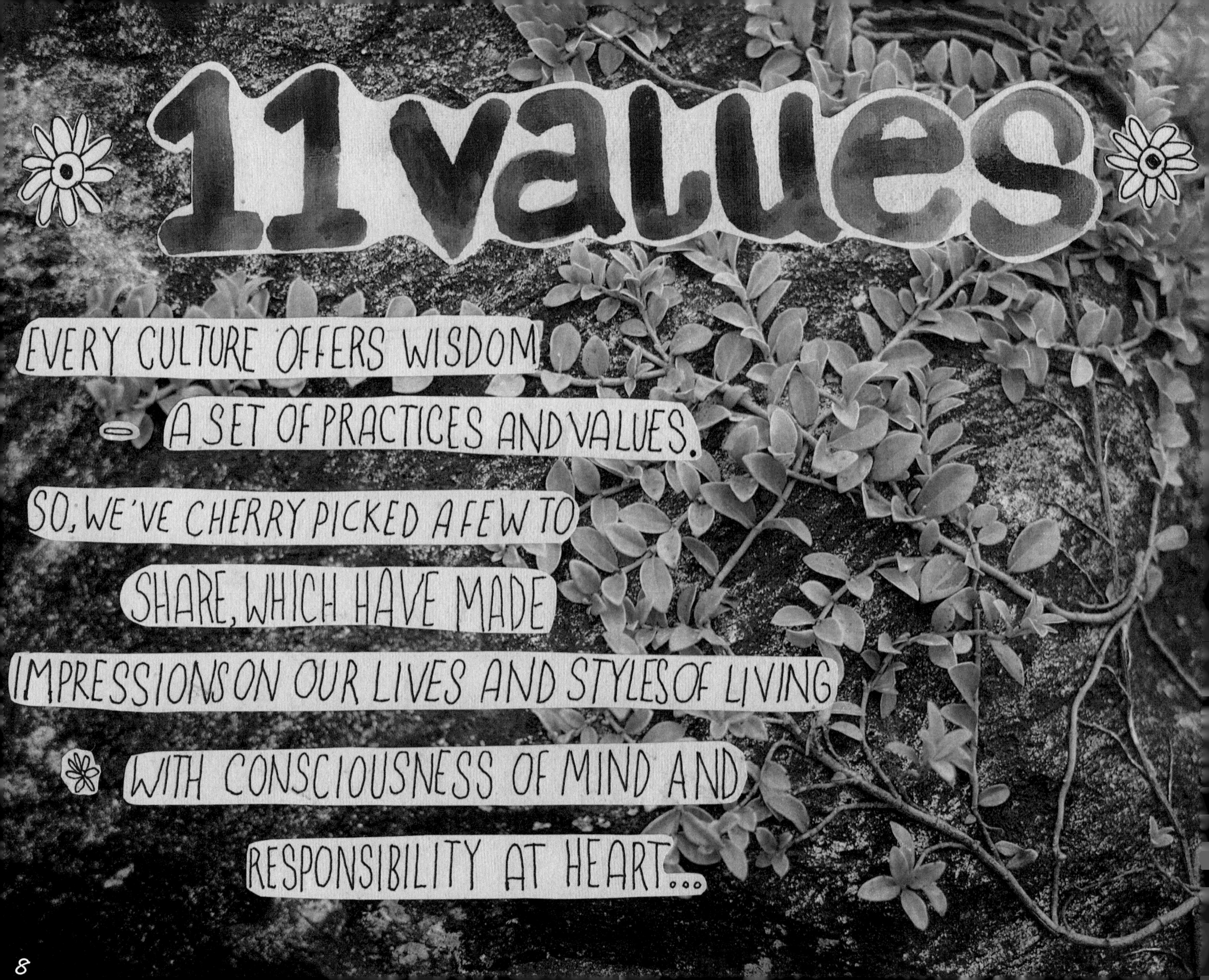
11 VALUES
EVERY CULTURE OFFERS WISDOM
- A SET OF PRACTICES AND VALUES.
SO, WE'VE CHERRY PICKED A FEW TO
SHARE, WHICH HAVE MADE
IMPRESSIONS ON OUR LIVES AND STYLES OF LIVING
WITH CONSCIOUSNESS OF MIND AND
RESPONSIBILITY AT HEART...

1. KEEP IT SIMPLE

LIKE ANIMALS IN THE WILD, WHO EAT ONLY ONE TYPE OF FOOD AT A TIME, OUR BODIES TOO ENJOY SIMPLICITY.

THROUGHOUT THE AGES, WE HAVE ROMANTICISED RICH, DENSE AND COMPLICATED FOODS.
IT HAS BECOME THE NORM TO COMBINE INGREDIENTS FROM ALL CORNERS OF THE GLOBE, WHICH WERE NEVER MEANT TO BE PAIRED. ALTHOUGH THIS CREATES DELICIOUS DISHES, OUR BODIES FIND IT INCREASINGLY DIFFICULT TO PROCESS ALL OF THIS INFORMATION IN JUST ONE SITTING.

IT MAY BE A STRETCH TO SIMPLIFY OUR MEALS TO JUST ONE, TWO OR THREE INGREDIENTS, BUT WE MUST MAKE A CONSCIOUS EFFORT TO CREATE MEALS THAT HELP OUR BODIES DIGEST THE FOOD WE GIVE IT.

SIMPLIFYING OUR MEALS MEANS LESS BLOATING, CLEARER CHANNELS, BETTER MOODS AND A HAPPIER GUT FOR ALL.

SOUNDS A DREAM HEY?

2. EAT NATURALLY

WE'VE BECOME SO ACCUSTOMED TO PACKAGED AND PROCESSED FOODS THAT WE NO LONGER ASK THE QUESTIONS 'WHAT'S IN IT?' AND 'WHAT WILL IT DO TO US?'

THE RISE IN PRESERVATIVES, COLOURINGS, FLAVOURINGS, AND OTHER 'NASTIES' HAS COME HAND-IN-HAND WITH A PANDEMIC OF CHRONIC ILLNESS AND WEIGHT-RELATED ISSUES.

FOR THOSE WHO DON'T KNOW, A PRESERVATIVE IS SOMETHING THAT PREVENTS THE NATURAL DECOMPOSITION OF FOOD. WHICH RAISES THE QUESTION - WHEN WE EAT THESE CHEMICALS, HOW DO THEY IMPACT OUR BODY'S NATURAL FUNCTIONING?

WE MAY NOT SEE THE EFFECT OF THESE CHEMICALS ON OUR BODILY SYSTEMS INITIALLY, BUT WITH TIME COMES HIDDEN ILLNESSES THAT CAN POTENTIALLY BE LIFE-LONG.

WHOLE AND NATURALLY PRESERVED FOODS ARE THE WAY FORWARD IF WE ARE TO HEAL THE DAMAGE DONE TO OUR GUTS. SIMPLY PUT - IF YOU CAN'T TELL WHAT AN INGREDIENT IS BY ITS NAME - THEN DON'T EAT IT.

Don't Panic, 3. It's Organic

Even though they've been used for years, we are only just beginning to see the effects of inorganic pesticide, herbicide and chemical use on our environment and bodies.

It is surfacing that chemicals, such as Glyphosate; the most commonly used global herbicide (also classed as an antibiotic), effectively immobilise our digestive systems over time. Studies show that these contribute to illnesses such as irritable bowel syndrome and autoimmune disorders.

Unbelievably, this stuff is sprayed all over the inorganic grains, vegetables and fruits that are making a home in your kitchen, and even seeps into our water systems. The only way to significantly reduce these chemicals in our lives is to opt for organic wherever possible.

If you can't grow, trade or buy fresh organic food, then at least make sure your staple oat, wheat, soy and rice products are organic - as these tend to hold the highest amount of contaminants.

4. Better Fresher

The longer food is kept and stored before being eaten, the less Prana, or 'life-force energy', it has.

Plants get their energy from the sun. Once they are harvested, the increasing process of entropy limits the amount of energy available within the plant for us to consume. You still get the 'calories', but the life-giving energy has effectively evacuated the building.

Additionally, our shop-bought vegetables and fruit are often already stored for a long time before our purchasing of them.

That's why we recommend keeping food for only a few days at most before eating it.

Eating food when it is still hot, instead of refrigerating and reheating it, enables you to receive and benefit from its most energetic state.

We advise against eating frozen, microwaved or packaged food, as these have effectively lost all of their vital energy.

5. GOOD TIMING, LESS WHINING

REGULAR MEALS ARE A MUST.
CONTRARY TO POPULAR BELIEF, OUR BODIES KNOW WHAT FOOD THEY NEED, AND EXACTLY WHEN TO EAT IT.

WE MUST LEARN TO LISTEN TO, AND EAT WITH, OUR BELLIES - NOT OUR MINDS.

ESTABLISHING A SOLID ROUTINE FOR EATING IS VITAL FOR OUR BODIES TO WORK OPTIMALLY. FOR MOST PEOPLE, THREE MEALS A DAY WORKS WELL - WITH THE LAST MEAL BEING THE LIGHTEST. IT CAN DO YOUR BODY WONDERS TO EAT AFTER SUN-RISE AND BEFORE SUN-DOWN, WHEN OUR DIGESTIVE FIRE BURNS BRIGHTER.

THE GOLDEN RULE
DON'T EAT TOO MUCH, AND DON'T EAT TOO LITTLE EITHER.

WE MUST LEARN AND LISTEN TO WHAT WORKS FOR OUR INDIVIDUAL, UNIQUE BODIES.

SO, BEGIN TO BUILD A RELATIONSHIP WITH YOUR BODY AND TAKE NOTE OF ITS SIGNALS, IT ONLY WANTS THE BEST FOR YOU!

6. LOVE - THE PROCESS

WE BELIEVE THE MOST IMPORTANT PART OF FOOD IS HOW IT'S CREATED, FROM SEED TO TABLE.

THERE IS SOMETHING TO LOVED FOOD THAT HAS BEEN GROWN, COOKED AND EATEN WITH CARE AND AWARENESS. IT NOURISHES THE PEOPLE WHO EAT IT IN WAYS WE CAN FEEL, BUT CANNOT YET MEASURE.

MANY ANCIENT TRADITIONS EMPHASISE THE IMPORTANCE OF LOVE IN FOOD PREPARATION. IN THE HINDU CULTURE, FOOD COOKED WITH LOVE IS PRASAD - IT CONTAINS BLESSINGS OF PRANA THAT THE RECIPIENT ABSORBS.

FOOD MADE BY FACTORIES, INSTEAD OF HANDS, IS VOID OF THIS LIFE-GIVING ENERGY AND CAN BE DETRIMENTAL TO OUR PATH TO HEALTH.

7. IMPRESSIONS ARE EVERYTHING...

ACCORDING TO ANCIENT SYSTEMS SUCH AS AYURVEDA, WE ARE IN OUR MOST IMPRESSIONABLE STATE WHEN WE ARE EATING.

WHILST FILLING OUR BELLIES, WE ARE ALSO INGESTING 'FOOD' AS SOUNDS THROUGH OUR EARS, SIGHTS THROUGH OUR EYES, TOUCH THROUGH OUR SKIN AND SMELLS THROUGH OUR NOSES.

IT IS IMPORTANT TO BE SAT IN A COMFORTABLE PLACE, WITH GOOD COMPANY AND LIGHT CONVERSATION (IF ANY), AND TO BE UNDISTURBED BY NOISES, TECHNOLOGY AND OTHER DISTRACTIONS WHILE WE NOURISH OUR BODIES WITH FOOD.

IF WE EAT FOODS WITH DISTURBED EMOTIONS AND SENSES, IT IS BELIEVED THAT EVEN THE HEALTHIEST OF FOOD CAN BECOME TOXIC, RATHER THAN HEALING TO US.

HENCE, THE IMPORTANCE OF 'MINDFUL EATING' - WHERE WE TAKE THE TIME TO BE PRESENT WITH THE FOOD THAT EVENTUALLY BECOMES US...
- TO TASTE, SMELL, AND ENJOY IT TO IT'S FULLEST.
AFTER ALL, WE ARE WHAT (AND HOW) WE EAT!

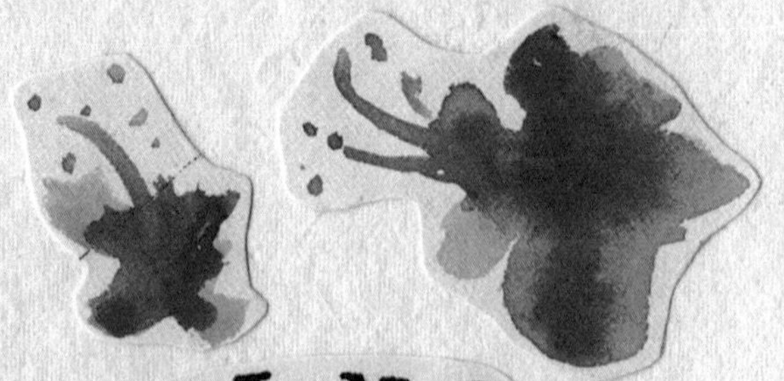

8. EVERYTHING IN MODERATION

WE NEED TO BE ABLE TO ENJOY A WHOLE RANGE OF DIFFERENT TASTES AND EXPERIENCES TO LIVE A LIFE OF BALANCE.

BUT WE OFTEN SUFFER FROM OVER-EMPHASISING JUST ONE TYPE OF FOOD, OR ONE TYPE OF EXPERIENCE.

AYURVEDA GUIDES US TO EXPLORE A RANGE OF THE DIFFERENT TASTES IN OUR LIVES - SWEET, SALTY, SOUR, PUNGENT AND ASTRINGENT, AND IN DOING SO, BRING OUR BODIES INTO BALANCE WITH OUR ENVIRONMENT.

IT IS IMPORTANT TO BE SOFT WITH TRANSITIONS IF YOU ARE MOVING OUT OF OLD, UNCONSCIOUS, AND USUALLY HARMFUL HABIT PATTERNS OF EATING AND LIFESTYLE PRACTICES, ESPECIALLY THOSE THAT PROVIDE A FEELING OF SAFETY AND COMFORT.

SO, PLEASE GO EASY AND BE GENTLE WITH YOURSELF ON THE ROAD OF CHANGE...AND REMEMBER TO GIVE YOURSELF A HUG EVERY NOW AND THEN.

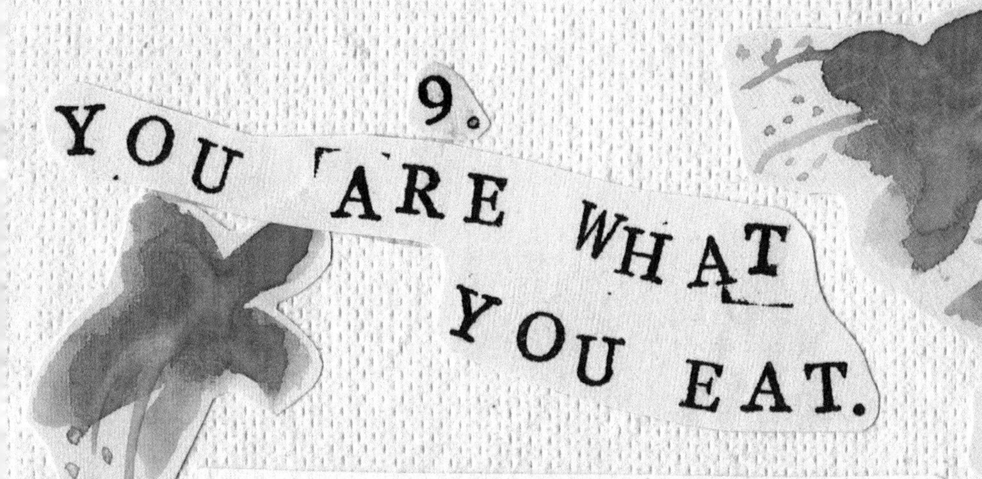

9. You are what you eat.

We've heard this one before...perhaps so much so that it has lost its poignant meaning.

And now, our ever-so-gracious modern agriculture practices have given 'you are what you eat' a whole new meaning.

Over the years, the 'advances' of animal farming have meant that eating meat and dairy usually means ingesting the natural and artificial hormones that are either injected into the animal, or produced by their nervous systems when they are suffering or being slaughtered.

When we eat animals, our bodies absorb and become everything that the animal has experienced too... and it can cause our mind, body and spirit great distress.

'Non-violence' is the first Yama (way of ethical living) in Yogic thought, and the eating of animals is considered to be violent, not only against the creatures involved, but against ourselves too.

10. Eat your environment

Worldwide, we are beginning to draw parallels between the micro-organisms in the soil and the ones in our human gut.
They are one and the same; our earth's soil is basically nature's gut!

Just like the friendly bacteria in our 'second brains', the bacteria in the soil intakes, digests and transforms organic matter into usable life-providing nutrients.

When we eat food that is grown locally and seasonally, we are effectively in-taking all of the beneficial bacteria and organisms we need to be well and have a healthy functioning gut.

We adapt to our environments by becoming them.
If you eat foods in the season that they are naturally available, then you are giving your body exactly what it needs to bring itself into balance in that particular climate.

By consciously eating with the seasons, you'll have more energy, clarity and will feel more nourished and connected.
What more could we ask for!

1|1. WHOLE WHOLE-FOODS

Overgrazing, mono-cropping and other unsustainable farming practices deplete the soil of nutrients. Soil depleted in nutrients produces food depleted in nutrients. Food depleted in nutrients produces humans depleted...you get the picture.

It is no wonder that we are seeing an abundance of deficiency-related problems in humans nowadays.

The health of our soil comes hand-in-hand with the health of our people - so it is extremely important that we recognise, implement and support regenerative farming i.e. agricultural practices that build the soil's nutritional value instead of deplete it!

'Whole whole-foods' are foods grown with

-LIFE-

in mind, by producers who care about both the land and the people who eat from it.

With only 60 years of arable top-soil left for farming globally, we need to change the way we grow, trade, buy and consume our food.

Love the planet and it will love you right back!

WE WOULD LIKE TO EMPHASISE HOW IMPORTANT IT IS NOT TO BE DOGMATIC WHEN IT COMES TO DIET. OFTEN THE MIND THINKS ONE THING, AND THE BODY FEELS ANOTHER.

WE FIND THE KEY LIES IN USING THE MIND TO SERVE THE BODY'S NEEDS. THEY ARE BOTH TOOLS AFTER ALL.

BE GENTLE WITH YOURSELF, AND EASE YOURSELF INTO ANY CHANGES.

Special Attention

We use various symbols to indicate if a dish is suitable for special dietary needs. These are as follows:

GF - Gluten Free

These foods are suitable for those intolerant to gluten. We are not, however, responsible for any cross-contamination that causes gluten to be present in your ingredients.

R - Raw

These recipes do not use heat to process any of the ingredients

S - Sprouted / Soaked

These recipes contain ingredients that are sprouted or soaked. Take note because they often need a few days to grow!

V - Vegan

These recipes are suitable for those avoiding eating animal products.

Vg - Vegetarian

This food is ok for those avoiding eating meat. The only animal product we use in the whole book is Honey.

F - Fermented

For recipes with fermented ingredients - good for the gut! When fermenting foods, make sure you check them frequently as they produce a lot of gas!

FOR GOOD MEASURE

WE UNDERSTAND THAT NOT EVERYONE USES THE METRIC SYSTEM, SO HERE ARE SOME EASY CONVERSIONS SO YOU DON'T HAVE TO WHIP YOUR GOOGLE OUT.

LIQID

WE USE MILLILITRES (ML)

10ML - 0.33 FL OZ
50ML - 1.69 FL OZ
100ML - 3.38 FL OZ
500ML - 16.9 FL OZ

TEMPERATURE

WE USE A FAN OVEN IN CELSIUS (°C)

120° C - 275° F - GAS 1
150° C - 325 ° F - GAS 3
160° C - 350° F - GAS 4
180° C - 400° F - GAS 5
200° C - 425° F - GAS 7
220° C - 475° F - GAS 9

WEIGHT

WE USE GRAMS (g)

5G - 0.18OZ
10G - 0.35OZ
50G - 1.76OZ
100G - 3.52OZ
500G - 17.63OZ

ODD MEASURES

WE USE HANDFULS AND SPRIGS FOR HERBS ECT. BUT ALL PEOPLE HAVE DIFFERENT SIZED HANDS, SO...

0.5 HANDFUL - 30G
1 HANDFUL - 60G
1 THUMB - 30G
1 SPRIG ROSEMARY - 1 TBSP LEAVES
1 SPRIG THYME - 0.5 TSP LEAVES

WHY WE ARE PICKY

THE FOLLOWING ARE SOME THINGS WE'RE PRETTY SERIOUS ABOUT, SO LISTEN UP!

FILTERED WATER

AS HUMANS, WE ARE OVER 70% WATER.
TO PUT THINGS SIMPLY, YOU DON'T WANT TO BUILD UP THE BULK OF YOUR BODY ON ANYTHING BUT THE BEST. EVEN 'SAFE' TAP WATER MAY HAVE HEAVY METALS AND EVEN CHLORINE IN IT, SO WE RECOMMEND GETTING A GOOD FILTER TO PULL THESE NASTIES OUT BEFORE ADDING TO THE RECIPES.

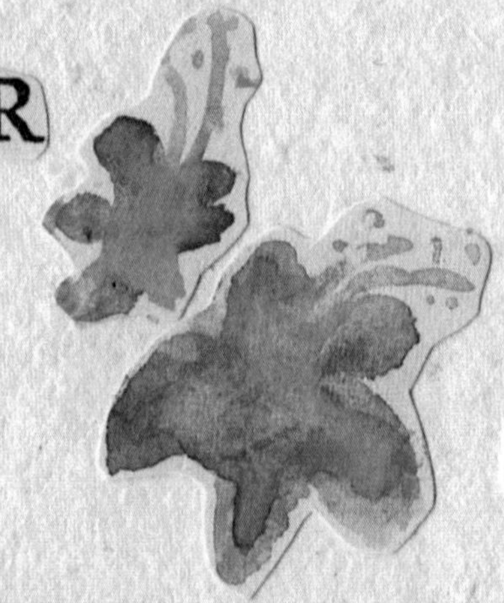

PACKAGED FOOD

WE TRY TO AVOID PACKAGED FOOD, BUT IF A RECIPE NEEDS IT, THEN MAKE SURE IT'S ORGANIC! IF YOU CAN'T GET ORGANIC, CHECK THE LABEL AND MAKE SURE THERE ARE NO CHEMICALS IN IT! YOU WOULDN'T BELIEVE IT, BUT THESE NASTY CHEMICALS ARE DISGUISED WITH ALL SORTS OF NAMES, LIKE 'NATURAL FLAVOURS', 'E212' AND ALL SORTS OF JARGON.
KEEP IT NATURAL AND THANK US LATER!

COCO-NUT OIL

NOT ALL OIL IS MADE EQUALLY.
COCONUT OIL DOESN'T DE-NATURE WHEN HEATED LIKE OTHER OILS DO. IT'S ALSO A WONDER FOOD AND DOES MANY MARVELLOUS THINGS TO MAKE THE BODY FUNCTION BETTER.

HIMALAYAN SALT

CONVENTIONAL TABLE SALT HAS 2 MINERALS IN IT - SODIUM AND CHLORIDE. HIMALAYAN SALT HAS 84 - ALL OF WHICH ARE USED BY OUR BODY FOR ESSENTIAL LIFE PROCESSES.
NEED WE ANY MORE EXPLANATION?

KEEP IT CLEAN

WE DON'T MENTION IT IN THE INDIVIDUAL RECIPES, BUT YOU SHOULD ALWAYS GIVE YOUR FRUIT AND VEG A GOOD WASH BEFORE USING IT. WE USUALLY SOAK OURS IN APPLE CIDER VINEGAR AND WARM, FILTERED WATER FIRST. IF IT AIN'T ORGANIC, IT'S GOOD TO SCRUB/PEEL IT TOO.

A LITTLE
BIT ABOUT...

AYURVEDA

Ayurveda is a very complex, ancient Vedic system of integrated healing for the mind, body and soul. It literally means 'Life Science' in Sanskrit.

With roots in India, Ayurveda covers everything from food, yoga asana and mantra to gem therapy and more. It may seem far-out, but with a little bit of belief, and a whole lot of love, it works. Take what feels right for you and integrate it into your own, beautifully unique way of living, sharing and collective healing.

The lifestyle and dietary recommendations that Ayurveda has offered us has been truly inspirational for both of us to balance and heal parts of ourselves we were previously unaware of. We would like to bow in utmost gratitude towards the Indian culture and teachers for providing the wisdom that has guided us to create this book. Naturally, we feel called to share what has helped us, and lend a hand on your journey if you wanted to do the same.

What we share in this book is only a glimpse of a much bigger picture, with an effort to make the information as simple and approachable as possible.

Ayurveda is a journey in itself, inwards and outwards. All it takes is a thirst for life and a want to take back your health into your own hands.

BASIC PRINCIPLES

AYURVEDA' S BASIC TEACHING IS THAT ALL LIFE IS INTERDEPENDENT; WE ARE ALL INTRINSICALLY CONNECTED WITH OUR ENVIRONMENT, AND SO, ANY CHANGES IN OUR ENVIRONMENT AND THE WAY WE EAT WILL CAUSE CHANGES IN US.

WE CAN SUMMARISE ITS TEACHINGS WITH THE FOLLOWING TWO PRINCIPLES

LIKE -INCREASES- LIKE

THE FACTORS IN OUR LIFE THAT HAVE A SIMILAR NATURE TO HEALTH - LIKE REST, GOOD FOOD, PEACE OF MIND AND MEDITATION - WILL INCREASE HEALTH.

ANY FACTORS THAT OPPOSE HEALTH - LIKE BAD DIET, STRESS AND OVER-WORK - DECREASE HEALTH.

THROUGH PROMOTING POSITIVE, LIFE-AFFIRMING FACTORS IN OUR LIVES, AND DECREASING THEIR OPPOSITES, WE CAN LIVE MORE IN HARMONY.

OPPOSITES CURE EACHOTHER

IN AYURVEDA, WE CAN INTRODUCE OPPOSITE QUALITIES TO OUR LIVES TO BALANCE THE CONDITIONS OF OUR HEALTH.

FOR EXAMPLE, AN EXCESS OF HEAT IN THE BODY WOULD REQUIRE THE OPPOSITE, THE APPLICATION OF COOLNESS, IN ORDER TO RESTORE BALANCE.

THIS APPLIES TO FOOD TOO. FOR EXAMPLE, IF WE EXPERIENCE HEART BURN FROM AN OVERLY SPICY MEAL, WE WOULD NEED TO CONSUME COOLING FOODS, AND AVOID IN-TAKING ANY MORE FIERY FOODS TO BRING OUR BODY BACK TO BALANCE.

THE ELEMENTS

AYURVEDA'S WISDOM IS CENTRED AROUND THE IDEA THAT WE, LIKE NATURE AROUND US, ARE BUILT OF AND FLUCTUATE BETWEEN 5 BASIC ELEMENTS:

EARTH

PROVIDES DENSITY IN OUR BONES, NAILS AND TEETH

AS OXYGEN IN OUR BREATH, FUELLING THE RESPIRATORY SYSTEM AND NERVES

AIR

FIRE

RELATES TO THE EYES (PERCEPTION) AND BODY HEAT

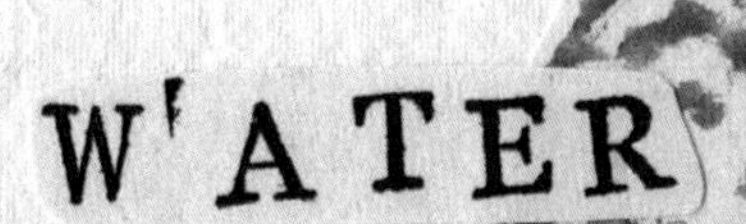

WATER

PROTECTS THE BODY THROUGH ITS FLUIDS, SUCH AS IN SALIVA, JOINTS AND DIGESTIVE JUICES

ETHER

CONNECTS THE EMPTY SPACES WITHIN OUR BODIES

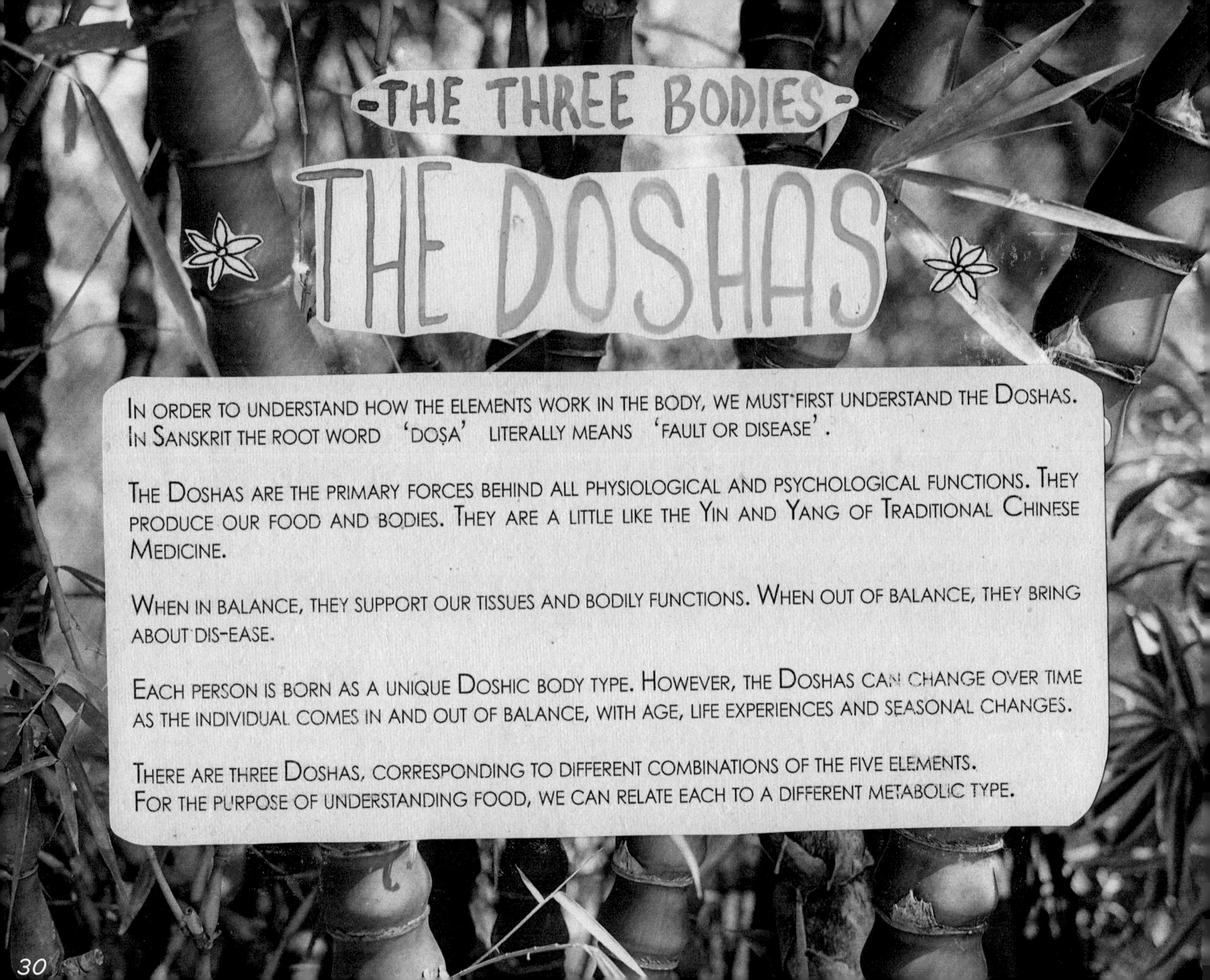

-The Three Bodies-

The Doshas

In order to understand how the elements work in the body, we must first understand the Doshas. In Sanskrit the root word ‘doṣa’ literally means ‘fault or disease’.

The Doshas are the primary forces behind all physiological and psychological functions. They produce our food and bodies. They are a little like the Yin and Yang of Traditional Chinese Medicine.

When in balance, they support our tissues and bodily functions. When out of balance, they bring about dis-ease.

Each person is born as a unique Doshic body type. However, the Doshas can change over time as the individual comes in and out of balance, with age, life experiences and seasonal changes.

There are three Doshas, corresponding to different combinations of the five elements. For the purpose of understanding food, we can relate each to a different metabolic type.

PITTA

FIRE & WATER

PASSION
&
DIGESTION

AIR & ETHER

NERVOUSNESS
&
CREATIVITY

KAPHA

WATER & EARTH

INACTIVITY
&
CALMNESS

WHAT DOSHIC TYPE ARE YOU?

A person may be a single, dual, or, in rare occasions, all three Doshic types, depending on their attributes.

Although, people will almost always have a predominant Dosha, followed by a secondary Dosha.

The questionnaire on the following page will help you to determine your Doshic type.
For mixed Doshic types, it is good to balance the Doshas seasonally.

The Questionnaire:

You only need to do the questionnaire once to find out your predominant Dosha.

Answer the questions as honestly as possible.

It can help to get somebody who knows you well to fill it out for you to get a second opinion.

Interpretation of Results:

If you are score highly on one Dosha (eg. V20 P8 K3), then you' d be VATA (V)

If you score highly on two Doshas (eg. V11 P13 K7), then you' d be PITTA-VATA (PV)

If you score evenly across the board (eg. V10 P10 K11), then you' d be V-P-K (VPK)

7 Doshic Types:

1. VATA
2. PITTA
3. KAPHA
4. VATA-PITTA
5. PITTA-KAPHA
6. VATA-KAPHA
7. VATA-PITTA-KAPHA

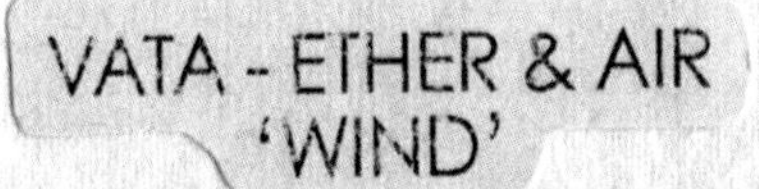

VATA - ETHER & AIR
'WIND'

'THAT WHICH MOVES THINGS'

QUALITIES:
COLD, LIGHT, DRY, ROUGH, FLOWING, SPACIOUS

ROLE: NERVOUS SYSTEM
(SENSORY AND MENTAL BALANCE, MOTOR ORIENTATION, COMPREHENSION)

PITTA - FIRE & WATER
'BILE'

'THAT WHICH DIGESTS THINGS'

QUALITIES:
HOT, LIGHT, SHARP, OILY, LIQUID, MOBILE

ROLE: CHEMICAL AND METABOLIC TRANSFORMATION
(MENTAL DIGESTION, PERCEPTION, UNDERSTANDING)

KAPHA - WATER & EARTH
'PHLEGM'

'THAT WHICH HOLDS THINGS TOGETHER'

QUALITIES:
STABLE, HEAVY, SLOW, COLD, SOFT, DULL

ROLE: NOURISHMENT AND SUBSTANCE
(EMOTIONAL SUPPORT, LOVE, COMPASSION, FORGIVENESS)

THE QUESTIONNAIRE

TICK THE BOX THAT APPLIES FOR EACH ATTRIBUTE AND CALCULATE YOUR TOTALS AT THE BOTTOM TO DETERMINE YOUR DOSHIC TYPE

	VATA		PITTA		KAPHA	
BASIC BODILY STRUCTURE						
FRAME	Tall, short or thin Poorly developed physique		Medium Moderately developed physique		Stout, stocky, short Big, well-developed physique	
WEIGHT	Light, hard to hold weight Prominent veins & bones		Moderate, Good muscles		Heavy Tends towards obesity	
COMPLEXION	Dull, brown, darkish		Red, ruddy, flushed, glowing		White, pale	
SKIN, TEXTURE & TEMPERATURE	Thin, dry, cold, rough, cracked, Prominent veins		Warm, moist, pink, with moles, freckles, acne		Thick, white, moist, cold, soft, smooth	
HAIR	Scanty, coarse, dry, brown, slightly wavy		Moderate, fine, soft, early grey or bald		Abundant, oily, thick, very wavy, lustrous	
FACE	Thin, small, long, wrinkled, dusky, dull		Moderate, ruddy, sharp contours		Large, round, fat, white or pale, soft contours	
NECK	Thin, long		Medium		Large, thick	
EYES	Small, dry, thin, brown, dull, unsteady		Medium, thin, red (inflamed easily), green, piercing		Wide, prominent, thick, oily, white, attractive	
LIPS	Thin, small, darkish, dry, unsteady		Medium, soft, red		Thick, large, oily, smooth, firm	
TEETH & GUMS	Thin, dry, small, rough, crooked, receding gums		Medium, soft, pink, gums bleed easily		Large, thick, soft, pink, oily	
CHEST	Thin, small, narrow, poorly developed		Medium		Broad, large, well or overly developed	
HANDS	Small, thin, dry, rough, fissured, unsteady		Medium, warm, pink		Large, thick, oily, cool, firm	
THIGHS	Thin, narrow		Medium		Well-developed, round, fat	
JOINTS	Small, thin, dry, unsteady, cracking		Medium, soft, loose		Large, thick, well-built	
NAILS	Small, thin, dry, rough, fissured, cracked, darkish		Medium, soft, pink		Large, thick, smooth, white, firm, oily	

WASTE MATERIALS / METABOLISM						
URINE	Scanty, difficult, colourless		Profuse, yellow, red, burning		Moderate, whitish, milky	
FECES	Scanty, dry, hard, difficult or painful, gas, tends towards constipation		Abundant, loose, sometimes yellowish, tends towards diarrhoea, with burning sensation		Moderate, solid, sometimes pale in colour, mucus in stool	
SWEAT / BODY ODOR	Scanty, no smell		Profuse, hot, strong smell		Moderate, cold, pleasant smell	
APPETITE	Variable, sharp		Strong, sharp		Constant, low	
CIRCULATION	Poor, variable, erratic		Good, warm		Slow, steady	
GENERAL CHARACTERISTICS						
TYPE OF ACTIVITY	Quick, fast, unsteady, erratic, hyperactive		Medium, motivated, purposeful, goal seeking		Slow, steady, stately	
STRENGTH / EXERTION	Low, poor endurance, starts & stops quickly		Medium, intolerant of heat		Strong, good endurance, but slow in starting	
RESISTANCE TO DISEASE	Poor, variable, weak immune system		Medium, prone to infections		Good, consistent, strong immune system	
DISEASE TENDENCY	Nervous system diseases, pain, arthritis, mental disorders		Febrile diseases, infections, inflammatory diseases		Respiratory system diseases, mucus, edema	
MENTAL FACTORS & EXPRESSION						
VOICE	Low, weak, hoarse		High pitch, sharp		Pleasant, deep, good tone	
SPEECH	Quick, inconsistent, erratic, talkative		Moderate, argumentative, convincing		Slow, definite, not talkative	
MENTAL NATURE	Quick, adaptable, indecisive		Intelligent, penetrating, critical, logical		Slow, steady, deep, dull	
EMOTIONAL TENDENCIES	Fearful, anxious, nervous		Angry, irritable, contentious		Calm, content, attached, sentimental	
FAITH	Erratic, changeable, rebel		Determined, fanatic, leader		Constant, loyal, conservative	
SLEEP PATTERNS	Light, tends towards insomnia		Moderate, may wake up but will fall asleep again		Heavy, difficult in waking up	
HABITS	Likes moving, travelling, parks, plays, jokes, stories, artistic activities, dancing		Likes competitive sports, politics, debates, hunting		Likes water, sailing, flowers, cosmetics, cooking	
TOTAL						

THE DOSHAS AND DIET

BELOW IS A BRIEF GUIDELINE ON THE TYPE OF FOODS EACH DOSHIC TYPE COULD OPT FOR, OR AVOID, TO MAINTAIN BALANCE AND OPTIMAL HEALTH.

HERE WE MUST REMEMBER THE *'OPPOSITES CURE EACH-OTHER'* PRINCIPLE, WHERE A PERSON WITH A DOSHA THAT IS OUT-OF-BALANCE CAN CONSUME FOODS WITH THE OPPOSING QUALITIES OF THE TWO OTHER DOSHAS IN ORDER TO COME BACK TO HARMONY.

VATA

TO EAT:

WARM, MOIST, AND SOFT FOODS (E.G. BERRIES, BANANAS, PEACHES, COOKED VEGGIES, OATS, BROWN RICE)

TO AVOID:

BITTER, DRIED, AND COLD FOODS (E.G. RAW VEGETABLES, COLD DESSERTS, DRIED FRUITS)

PITTA

TO EAT:

LIGHT, COLD, SWEET, AND ENERGIZING FOODS (E.G. FRUITS, NON-STARCHY VEGETABLES, OATS)

TO AVOID:

HEAVY, SPICY, AND SOUR FOODS (E.G. RED MEAT, WHITE POTATOES, HOT SPICES)

KAPHA

TO EAT:

SPICY, ACIDIC, AND LIGHT FOODS (E.G. MOST FRUITS AND VEGETABLES, WHOLE GRAINS, HOT SPICES)

TO AVOID:

HEAVY, "FATTY" FOODS (E.G. FATS, OILS, PROCESSED FOODS, NUTS, SEEDS)

* THESE ARE VERY BRIEF GUIDELINES AND ARE JUST TO GIVE AN IDEA OF THE DIETS TO BALANCE EACH DOSHIC TYPE. WE RECOMMEND DOING A BIT MORE RESEARCH INTO THE COMPLEX FOOD LISTS THAT AYURVEDA RECOMMENDS FOR EACH BODY TYPE, THEN EATING BECOMES AN ART!

OUT OF BALANCE DOSHAS

The following symptoms may occur if a particular Dosha becomes out of balance in the body through excessive lifestyle choices, such as eating unsuitable foods for the current season.

Here we must remember the *'like increases like'* principle where, for example, a person predominant in the vata Dosha may have eaten too much gas-forming, raw food, causing an imbalance which, over time, may cause disease.

HIGH VATA (WIND)

EMACIATION
DEBILITY, SEEKING WARMTH
TREMORS
DISTENTION AND CONSTIPATION
INSOMNIA
SENSORY PROBLEMS
DIZZINESS
CONFUSION
NERVOUSNESS

HIGH PITTA (HEAT)

YELLOW COLOUR STOOL OR URINE
YELLOW COLOUR EYES OR SKIN
HUNGER
THIRST
BURNING SENSATIONS
DIFFICULTY SLEEPING
AGITATION
FRUSTRATION
ANGER

HIGH KAPHA (STAGNANCY)

LOW DIGESTIVE FIRE
NAUSEA
LETHARGY
HEAVINESS
CHILLS
LOOSENESS OF LIMBS
COUGH
DIFFICULTY BREATHING
EXCESSIVE SLEEPING

* This book is only a supplement to an already healthy lifestyle. If you have any of these symptoms and they are worsening, we recommend you seek professional help from a medical expert!

USING THE DOSHAS IN THIS BOOK

YOU' LL NOTICE 'V', 'P' AND 'K' ON EACH PAGE WITH A '~', '-' OR '+' NEXT TO THEM.

THESE REFER TO EACH DOSHA - VATA (V), PITTA (P) AND KAPHA (K). COMPLETE THE QUESTIONNAIRE TO DETERMINE YOUR DOSHIC TYPE AND THEN USE THIS METHOD TO DETERMINE WHAT RECIPES WOULD BE BEST FOR YOU AT ANY GIVEN MOMENT.

THE IDEA IS TO EAT TO BALANCE YOUR DOSHA. FOR EXAMPLE:

DOSHIC TYPE	HEALING APPROACH
VATA	VATA PACIFYING
PITTA	PITTA PACIFYING
KAPHA	KAPHA PACIFYING
VATA-PITTA	KAPHA INCREASING
VATA-KAPHA	PITTA INCREASING
PITTA-KAPHA	VATA INCREASING
VATA-PITTA-KAPHA	TREAT SPECIFIC SYMPTOMS & ATTRIBUTES

YOU' LL FIND THAT YOU FEEL DIFFERENT EVERY DAY AS YOUR BODY COMES IN AND OUT OF BALANCE DEPENDING ON YOUR ENVIRONMENT, SEASONS, ACTIVITY ETC.

FOR EXAMPLE, A PERSON PREDOMINANT IN KAPHA MAY BE FEELING UNGROUNDED, NERVOUS OR BLOATED. IN THIS CASE, THEY WOULD NEED TO EAT VATA PACIFYING (V~ OR V-) FOODS.

FOR SIMPLICITIES SAKE, WE CAN SAY THAT:
YOU HAVE A GENERAL DOSHIC TYPE, BY NATURE.
BUT THIS CAN FLUCTUATE DAILY DEPENDING ON YOUR ENVIRONMENT.

WE ENCOURAGE YOU TO FEEL INTO WHAT YOU MIND AND BODY NEEDS.

THE SEASONS

Each Dosha has its corresponding season. This means that we need to look at eating foods the can help balance out the effects of different weather and climates.

Each recipe page in this book suggests the general season that each meal can be eaten in. Again, this will vary by your individual Doshic constitution.

The Doshas have their seasons as follows:

Kapha Season: Late Winter and Early Spring
Pitta Season: Late Spring and Summer
Vata Season: Autumn and Early Winter

VATA

In Vata season we experience drier and cooler weather, so we can opt for a diet that is Vata pacifying (V~ or V-) with foods that are more warming, moistening, nutritive and heating (P+ or K+).

PITTA

In Pitta season we experience hotter and drier weather, so we could opt for a Pitta pacifying diet (P~ or P-), with predominantly moist, cooling and light (V+ or K+) to stop us from over-heating due to excess heat.

KAPHA

In Kapha season we experience a damper environment, meaning we could eat a diet predominantly Kapha pacifying (K~ or K-) with Pitta increasing (P+) heating and Vata increasing (V+) drying foods to 'burn up' the stagnant/damp Kapha in the body.

-THE THREE QUALITIES-  THE GUNAS 

Ayurveda teaches us that nature is composed of three prime energetic qualities, the Gunas. The word 'Gunas' means 'what binds'. All parts of nature exhibit qualities of one or more of the Gunas, which have an effect on our body and mind.

For the purpose of this book, we will explore how different foods have the qualities of Sattva, Rajas, or Tamas, and how these qualities, when consumed, can effect our physical and mental states.

SATTVA

Principle of intelligence

Quality: stability, harmony, virtue

Nature: light, luminous

Brings about: awakening and development of the soul

Creates: happiness

RAJAS

Principle of energy

Quality: distraction, turbulence, activity

Nature: mobile, motivated

Brings about: self-motivated and self-seeking action

Creates: pain, suffering and energy

TAMAS

Principle of materiality

Quality: dullness, darkness, inertia

Nature: heavy, veiling, obstructing

Brings about: decay, degeneration and death

Creates: delusion

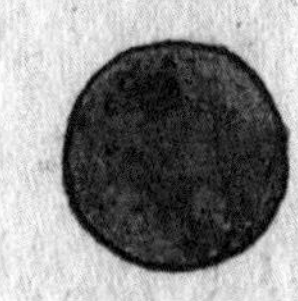

Sattva is the highest quality, which can lead us to self-realisation of our true nature.

Rajas causes dissipation of energy, which eventually causes Tamas, bringing about decay and death.

The aim of Ayurvedic and Yogic practices and healing is to attain a predominant quality of Sattva in our lives, named 'pure Sattva'.

The qualities of Rajas and Tamas can cause disease, and so, within Ayurvedic thought, it is optimal for our well-being to aim for a diet and lifestyle consisting of mainly Sattvic foods and experiences, which harmonise the body and mind.

Here are some examples of different food and lifestyle types of each Guna

SATTVIC

FOOD

- Fresh fruits and veggies
- Fresh leafy veggies
- Moderate use of spices
- Grains such as rice, wheat, barley, maize
- Raw soaked seeds and nuts
- Fresh, raw milk
- Sweeteners like honey and jaggery

LIFESTYLE

Meditative activity, conserves energy, understands body and mind, harmony with life

RAJASIC

FOOD

- Overly spicy, salty, sour and tasty food
- Onion and garlic
- Pungent vegetables
- Fried and salted foods
- Chillies, pickles and vinegar
- Alcoholic and soft drinks
- Coffee and black tea
- Excess cabbage, broccoli and cauliflower

LIFESTYLE

Excessive activity, lack of focus, a lot of sexual activity, mental agitation

TAMASIC

FOOD

- Stale and reheated food
- Oily and heavy food
- Food with artificial preservatives and additives
- Canned, tinned or preserved food
- Meat and fish
- Pasteurised milk, curds and cheese
- Excess fats, oils, sugars, pastries
- White sugar and white flour

LIFESTYLE

Sedentary, depressed state, lack of motivation, overly attached

THE DIGESTIVE FIRE

It is very important to understand the concept of Agni, our digestive fire, when creating and eating food that is based on Ayurvedic principles.

Agni is effectively our body's 'furnace', to transform and produce usable energy from the food and drink we consume.

The word 'Agni' means *'to burn, transform or perceive'*, having the qualities of fire.

It is increased by like-natured foods, such as ginger, black pepper and cayenne or hot and spicy foods.

Agni requires fuel to burn, like an oil lamp. The idea is- when the oil is sufficient and burning optimally, toxins will be burnt away and not accumulated in our body, our minds and senses will in turn be clear and sharp.

Without toxic build up, our bodies can work harmoniously with the nature around us, self-regulating to life's changing nature.

On the other hand, when Agni is weak and deficient, we suffer from heaviness, dullness, cloudy emotions and general stagnation in our lives.

It is important to learn to sense if our digestive fire is working correctly, and to take measures to enhance it if needed.

HOW AGNI OPPERATES IN EACH DOSHA

VATA

GENERALLY HAVE VARIABLE AGNI

NERVOUS DIGESTION

FLUCTUATE FROM VERY HUNGRY TO NOT HUNGRY

AGNI CAN BE IRRITATED BY FASTING

PITTA

GENERALLY HAVE HIGH AGNI

STRONG APPETITE AND DIGESTION

DO NOT GAIN EXCESSIVE WEIGHT

AGNI CAN BE IRRITATED BY FASTING

KAPHA

GENERALLY HAVE LOW AGNI

LOW BUT CONSTANT APPETITES

SLOW METABOLISM

HOLD ON TO WEIGHT EASILY

AGNI BENEFITS FROM FASTING

WAYS TO STIMULATE AGNI

- EAT HEATING FOODS, HERBS AND SPICES
- REGULAR AEROBIC EXERCISE (UNTIL SWEAT FORMS ON FOREHEAD)
- AVOID EATING PRE-SUNRISE OR POST-SUNSET
- REDUCE DRINKING COLD BEVERAGES
- EAT UNTIL YOU ARE TWO-THIRDS FULL
- EAT WHEN HUNGRY
- BELLY MASSAGES

WHEN ALL THREE DOSHAS AND EMOTIONS ARE BALANCED, AGNI IS BALANCED.

PRANA
-THE LIFE FORCE ENERGY-

-PRANA-

PRANA, ALSO KNOWN AS *'CHI'* IN TRADITIONAL CHINESE MEDICINE, IS OUR 'LIFE-FORCE ENERGY'.

ALL OF NATURE'S ENERGY ORIGINATES FROM THE SUN AND IS PASSED DOWN IN STAGES OF THE FOOD CHAIN, THROUGH PLANTS IN THE PROCESS OF PHOTOSYNTHESIS AND THEN TO US AND OTHER ANIMALS WHO EAT THOSE PLANTS.

THEREFORE, IT IS TAUGHT THAT CHOOSING AND CONSUMING FOOD WITH THE HIGHEST AMOUNT OF ENERGY WILL BE MOST BENEFICIAL TO OUR WELL-BEING.

THE FOODS WE EAT CAN DO ONE OF THREE THINGS:

1. IGNITE THE LIFE ENERGY WITHIN YOU (POSITIVE PRANA)
2. MAKE YOU LETHARGIC / SEDENTARY (NEUTRAL PRANA)
3. TAKE AWAY YOUR LIFE ENERGY AND VITALITY (NEGATIVE PRANA)

THE ENERGY OF OUR FOOD IS ADDITIONALLY INFLUENCED BY HOW IT IS COOKED AND EATEN. FOR EXAMPLE, PRANA CAN BE INCREASED OR DECREASED BY THE METHODS OF FOOD PREPARATION OR THE EMOTIONAL STATE OF THE COOK AND CONSUMER.

FOODS WITH...

POSITIVE PRANA

FRESH, SEASONAL FRUIT AND VEGGIES
MINIMALLY PROCESSED WHOLE GRAINS
LEGUMES
NUTS AND SEEDS
SPROUTED BEANS AND LEGUMES
CEREAL GRAINS

NEUTRAL PRANA

REFRIGERATED FRUIT AND VEGGIES
IMPORTED FRUIT AND VEGGIES
DRIED NUTS AND SEEDS
LEGUMES AND BEANS
POTATOES (EXCEPT FOR THE SWEET VARIETY, WHICH ARE ABUNDANT IN PRANA)
TOMATOES

NEGATIVE PRANA

EGGPLANTS
GREEN CHILLIS
COFFEE AND BLACK TEA
ALCOHOL
VINEGAR
MEAT
MICROWAVED FOOD
PROCESSED AND PACKAGED FOOD
FROZEN FOOD
CAFFEINE AND OTHER STIMULANTS

THROUGH THIS BOOK
WE HOPE YOU HAVE FOUND OUT
A LITTLE SOMETHING ABOUT

YOURSELF

AND YOUR CONNECTION TO

THE
BEAUTIFUL
WORLD
AROUND
YOU.

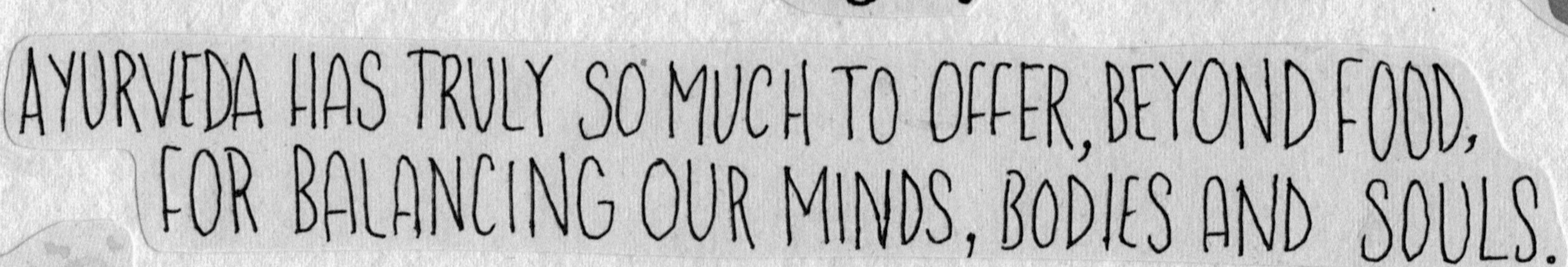

AYURVEDA HAS TRULY SO MUCH TO OFFER, BEYOND FOOD,
FOR BALANCING OUR MINDS, BODIES AND SOULS.

BUT FOR NOW... **LETTUCE EAT!**

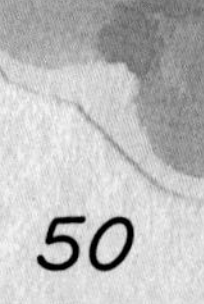

SPROUTING (ALMOST) ANYTHING

WHOLESOME WHOLEWHEAT PASTRY

SUPA GOLDEN PASTE

SUPA GREEN PASTE

ALMOND MILK

COCO-NATTY MILK

DATE CHUTNEY

PLANT PESTO

BLUEBERRY COMPOTE

IF YOU THOUGHT YOU KNEW YOUR 'SUPERFOODS', WELCOME TO A WHOLE NEW BALL PARK..!

SPROUTED FOODS

WHEN SPROUTED, A SEED'S LIFE FORCE (PRANA) IS 'ACTIVATED', WHICH MEANS THEY ARE JAM-PACKED WITH ENERGY FOR YOUR BENEFIT.

SPROUTS HAVE THE HIGHEST AMOUNT OF POTENTIAL ENERGY A FOOD CAN HAVE AS A RESULT OF THEIR TRANSFORMATION PROCESS FROM LITTLE SEEDS TO PLANTS!

SPROUTS

...YOUR CHOSEN DRY INGREDIENT

SOAK

... ACCORDING TO CHART TIMINGS.

DRAIN

... ONCE SOAKING IS COMPLETE

RINSE

...1-2 TIMES DAILY (DRY CLIMATE)
...3-4 TIMES DAILY (HUMID CLIMATE)

GIVE LOVE

SPROUT

... ACCORDING TO THE SPROUTING CHART TIMINGS.

SHARE AND ENJOY

... LOVE THE PEOPLE YOU LOVE BY FEEDING THEM SPROUTS.

YOU WILL NEED:

- 1 SPROUTING JAR WITH A MESH SPROUTING LID

OR

- 1 1L JAR WITH CLOTH AND RUBBER BAND
- 150g DRY GRAINS, SEEDS, LEGUMES OR BEANS (SEE CHART)

REMEMBER: LOVE YOUR FOOD AND IT WILL LOVE YOU BACK!

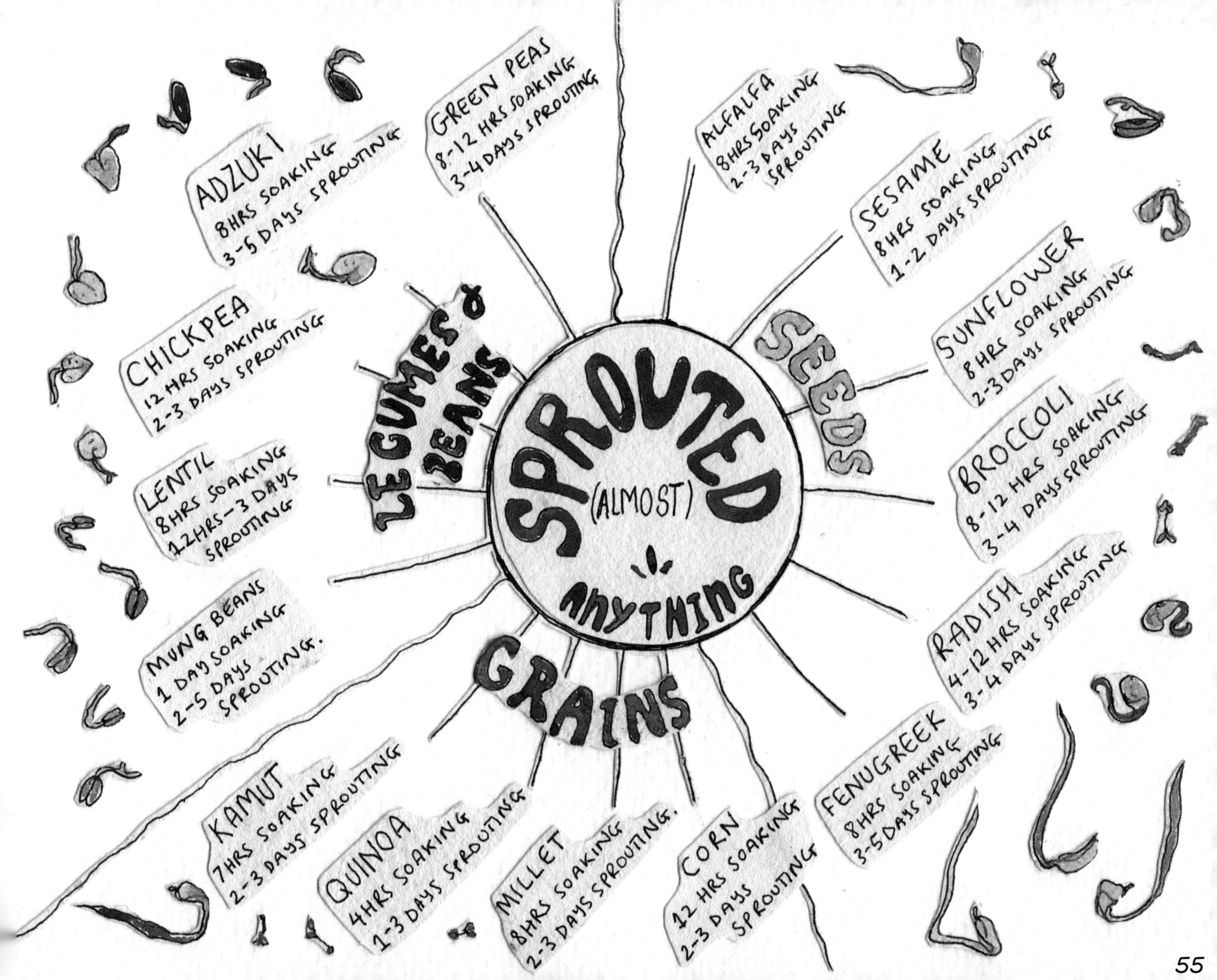
SPROUTED (ALMOST) ANYTHING
LEGUMES & BEANS
SEEDS
GRAINS
ADZUKI
8HRS SOAKING
3-5 DAYS SPROUTING
GREEN PEAS
8-12 HRS SOAKING
3-4 DAYS SPROUTING
ALFALFA
8HRS SOAKING
2-3 DAYS
SPROUTING
SESAME
8HRS SOAKING
1-2 DAYS SPROUTING
SUNFLOWER
8HRS SOAKING
2-3 DAYS SPROUTING
BROCCOLI
8-12 HRS SOAKING
3-4 DAYS SPROUTING
RADISH
4-12 HRS SOAKING
3-4 DAYS SPROUTING
FENUGREEK
8HRS SOAKING
3-5 DAYS SPROUTING
CORN
12 HRS SOAKING
2-3 DAYS
SPROUTING
MILLET
8HRS SOAKING
2-3 DAYS SPROUTING.
QUINOA
4HRS SOAKING
1-3 DAYS SPROUTING
KAMUT
7HRS SOAKING
2-3 DAYS SPROUTING
MUNG BEANS
1 DAY SOAKING
2-5 DAYS
SPROUTING.
LENTIL
8HRS SOAKING
12HRS-3 DAYS
SPROUTING
CHICKPEA
12 HRS SOAKING
2-3 DAYS SPROUTING

...BREATHE AND KNEAD,
BREATHE AND KNEAD...

BE PATIENT WITH THE CRUMBLING PROCESS AND WHEN KNEADING THE DOUGH. IT CAN TAKE SOME TIME TO GET THE TECHNIQUE RIGHT.

* PRACTICE MAKES PERFECT *

WHEN KNEADING THE DOUGH, USE A FLOURED SURFACE, OR A MIXING BOWL.

PASTRIES LIKE THIS ARE GOOD FOR VATA IN MODERATION AS THEY ARE GROUNDING AND NOURISHING. BUT WE MUST ALL BE CAREFUL TO NOT EAT TOO MUCH WHEAT AS IT TENDS TO CLOG OUR DIGESTIVE TRACTS.

WINTER, SUMMER, AUTUMN

40 MINUTES VP-K+

MAKES: 1 PIE OR 4 PASTIES

WHOLEWHEAT pastry

INGREDIENTS

400g ORGANIC WHOLEWHEAT FLOUR
0.5 TSP HIMALAYAN SALT
50mL COCONUT OIL
50mL OLIVE OIL
200mL FILTERED WATER.

METHOD

1. SIEVE THE FLOUR INTO A MIXING BOWL AND MIX WITH THE SALT.
2. IF NEEDED, MELT THE COCONUT OIL AND ADD IT, ALONG WITH THE OLIVE OIL TO THE MIXING BOWL. STIR THE OIL IN AND, WITH CLEAN HANDS, GENTLY CRUMBLE THE MIX BETWEEN YOUR FINGERS REPEATEDLY FOR 4 MINUTES. THIS SHOULD CREATE A BREAD-CRUMB CONSISTENCY. BE SURE TO REMOVE ALL LARGE LUMPS.
3. ADDING THE WATER, 50mL AT A TIME, USE A WOODEN SPOON TO STIR THE MIXTURE TOGETHER FOR AROUND 2 MINUTES - IT WILL BEGIN TO CLUMP. THEN KNEED THE MIX TOGETHER BY USING THE BALL OF YOUR HANDS TO PRESS THE DOUGH INTO THE WORK SURFACE, THEN FOLDING THE DOUGH IN HALF - REPEAT THIS PROCESS FOR UP TO 30 TIMES, OR UNTIL THE DOUGH IS AN ELASTIC CONSISTENCY. IT MAY FALL APART AT FIRST, SO BE PATIENT.
4. MOULD THE DOUGH INTO A BALL, PLACE IT IN THE MIXING BOWL AND COVER WITH A SLIGHTLY DAMP TEA TOWEL FOR 20 MINUTES.
5. WHEN READY, SPLIT THE DOUGH ACCORDING TO YOUR CHOSEN RECIPE'S INSTRUCTION, ROLL ONTO A FLOURED SURFACE AND ENJOY!

MAKES 3 curries FOR 4 PEOPLE · V · GF · VK-P+ · 20 MINUTES

Supa golden paste

INGREDIENTS

120g	FRESH GINGER ROOT
60g	FRESH TUMERIC ROOT
2	LIMES
12	GREEN HOT CHILLIS

4 TBSP	AGAVE NECTAR
0.5 CAN	ORGANIC COCONUT MILK
150 ML	FILTERED WATER
4 TBSP	COCONUT OIL.

18 PODS	CARDAMOM
3 TSP	CORIANDER SEEDS
3 TSP	CUMIN SEEDS
1 TSP	CARAWAY SEEDS
2 TSP	GROUND FENUGREEK
2 TSP	HOT CHILLI POWDER
2 TSP	PAPRIKA
0.25 TSP	ASAFOETIDA
1 TSP	CLOVES
3 PODS	STAR ANISE
2 TSP	HIMALAYAN SALT
2 TSP	BLACK PEPPER

METHOD

1. PEEL AND CHOP THE GINGER AND TUMERIC ROOT AND CHOP THE CHILLIS. ADD THESE INGREDIENTS TO A BLENDER.
2. LIGHTLY TOAST THE CORIANDER SEEDS, CUMIN SEEDS AND CARAWAY SEEDS IN A SMALL FRYING PAN FOR 1-2 MINUTES TO RELEASE THEIR AROMAS. THEN GRIND THESE WITH A PESTLE AND MORTAR. ADD THESE TO THE BLENDER.
3. IN THE PESTLE AND MORTAR, BASH THE CARDAMOM PODS TO RELEASE THEIR SEEDS, DISCARDING THE GREEN CASINGS. ADD THE SEEDS TO THE BLENDER.
4. SQUEEZE THE TWO LIMES INTO THE BLENDER AND ADD THE REMAINING INGREDIENTS. BLEND FOR 3 MINUTES UNTIL THE PASTE IS VERY SMOOTH.
5. SET ASIDE THE FINISHED PASTE INTO 3X 250ML JARS. STORE FOR UP TO 10 DAYS IN THE FRIDGE OR UP TO 6 MONTHS IN THE FREEZER.

20 MINUTES | MAKES 3 CURRIES FOR 4 PEOPLE | VPK ~

(V) (GF) (K)

Supa Green Paste

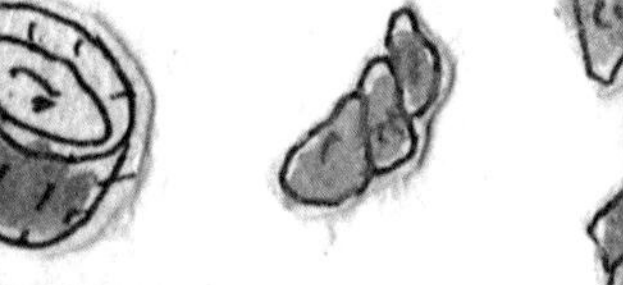
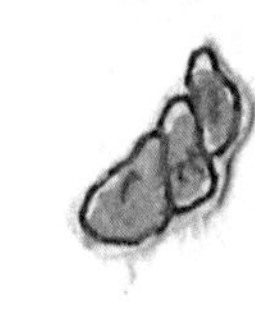
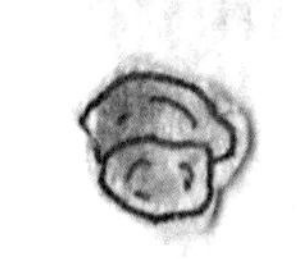

INGREDIENTS

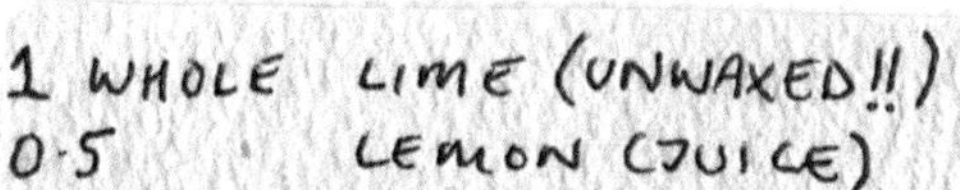

1 WHOLE	LIME (UNWAXED!!)
0·5	LEMON (JUICE)
6-7	THAI HOT CHILLIS
2 STICKS	LEMONGRASS
3 THUMBS	GINGER ROOT
3 THUMBS	GALANGAL ROOT
3 THUMBS	TUMERIC ROOT
1 GREEN	BELL PEPPER

3 TBSP	AGAVE NECTAR (OPTIONAL)
2 TBSP	COCONUT OIL
0·5 CAN	ORGANIC COCONUT MILK
200 ML	FILTERED WATER
1 TSP	GROUND CORIANDER SEEDS
1 TSP	GROUND CUMIN SEEDS
1 TSP	GROUND BLACK PEPPER
20g	FRESH THAI BASIL

METHOD

1. GRIND THE CUMIN AND CORIANDER WITH THE BLACK PEPPER IN A PESTLE AND MORTAR.

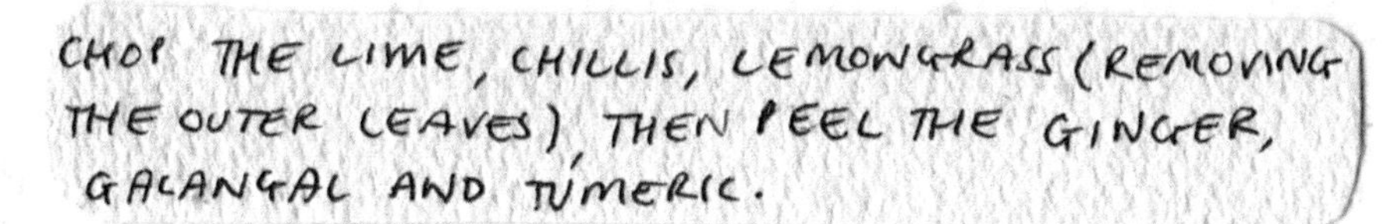

2. CHOP THE LIME, CHILLIS, LEMONGRASS (REMOVING THE OUTER LEAVES), THEN PEEL THE GINGER, GALANGAL AND TUMERIC.

3. ADD THESE INGREDIENTS, INCLUDING THE LIME RIND, TO A BLENDER OR FOOD PROCESSOR, ALONG WITH THE FRESH BASIL, LEMON JUICE, COCONUT OIL, COCONUT MILK, GROUND SEEDS AND BLACK PEPPER, AND THE OPTIONAL AGAVE NECTAR.
BLEND FOR 4 MINUTES, STIRRING OCCASIONALLY IF THE MIXTURE STICKS.

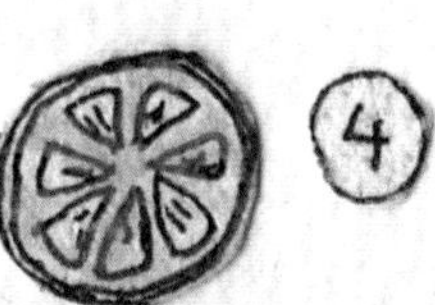

4. WHEN BLENDED, SET ASIDE THE PASTE INTO 3 JARS AND REFRIGERATE FOR LATER USE.
KEEP IN THE FRIDGE FOR UP TO 10 DAYS!
KEEP IN THE FREEZER FOR UP TO 6 MONTHS!

ACTIVATING YOUR ALMONDS HELPS TO BREAKDOWN ENZYME INHIBITORS AND PHYTIC ACID, WHICH RELEASES THE ENZYMES AND MAKES THE ALMONDS MUCH EASIER TO DIGEST AND EASIER ON THE TUMMY!
FYI!
IF YOU ARE USING SHOP BOUGHT PLANT MILK MAKE SURE YOU CHECK THE LABELS. IT IS VERY LIKELY YOUR FAVOURITE MILK HAS A TON OF ADDITIVES AS THICKENERS AND STABILISERS THAT DO NOT DO YOUR BODY ANY GOOD. KEEP IT NATURAL!

ALMOND

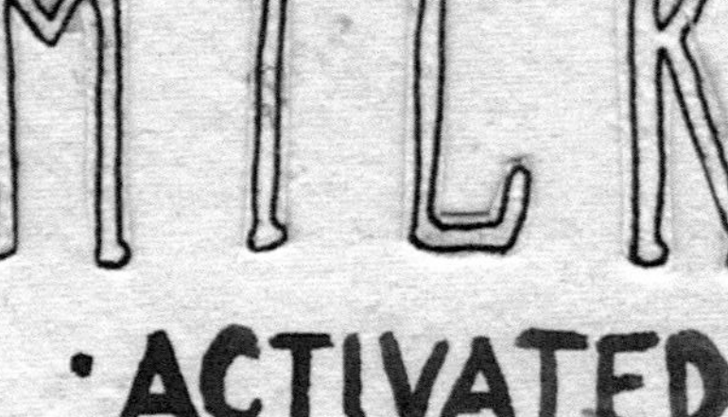

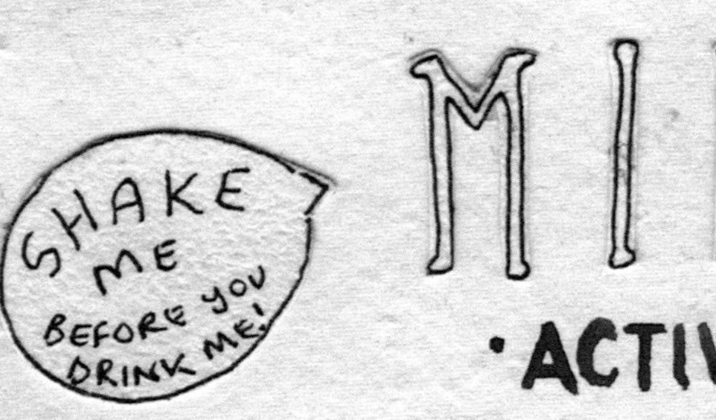

·ACTIVATED·

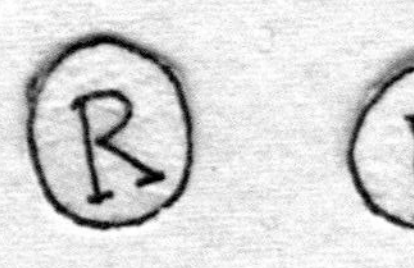

15 MINUTES

MAKES 500ML

INGREDIENTS

85g RAW ALMONDS
800ML FILTERED WATER
0.25 TSP CINNAMON
1 PINCH HIMALAYAN SALT

1. SOAK THE ALMONDS IN 300ML OF WARM WATER OVERNIGHT TO ACTIVATE THEM. THE FOLLOWING DAY, PEEL OFF THE SKINS AND DISCARD THEM.

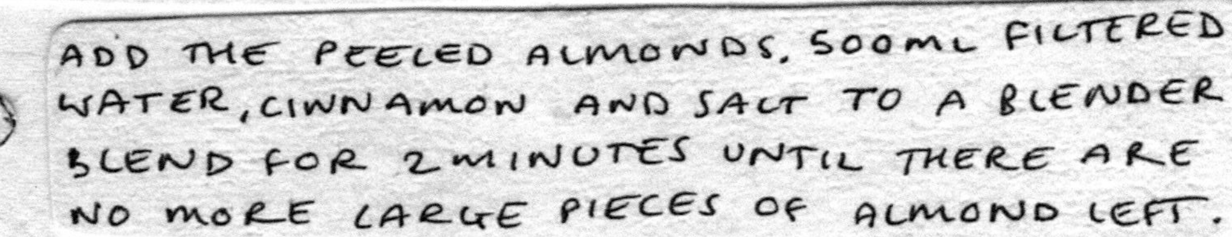

2. ADD THE PEELED ALMONDS, 500ML FILTERED WATER, CINNAMON AND SALT TO A BLENDER. BLEND FOR 2 MINUTES UNTIL THERE ARE NO MORE LARGE PIECES OF ALMOND LEFT.

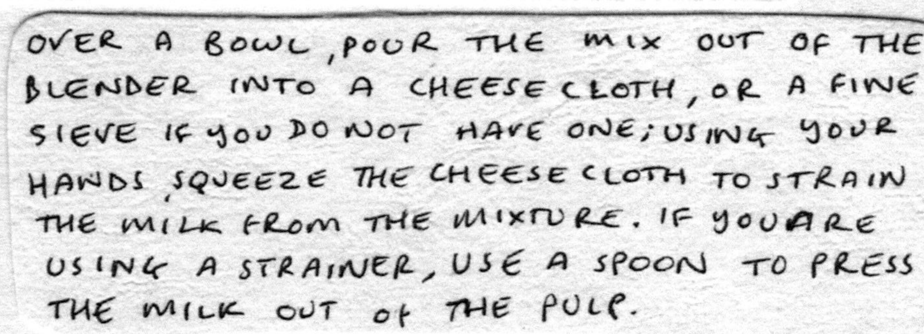

3. OVER A BOWL, POUR THE MIX OUT OF THE BLENDER INTO A CHEESECLOTH, OR A FINE SIEVE IF YOU DO NOT HAVE ONE; USING YOUR HANDS, SQUEEZE THE CHEESECLOTH TO STRAIN THE MILK FROM THE MIXTURE. IF YOU ARE USING A STRAINER, USE A SPOON TO PRESS THE MILK OUT OF THE PULP.

VPKN

4. WHEN DONE, POUR THE MILK INTO A 500ML BOTTLE AND REFRIGERATE FOR UP TO 3 DAYS.

ALL YEAR ROUND

* YOU CAN REFRIGERATE AND USE THE ALMOND PULP FOR UP TO 3 DAYS AND ADD IT TO DESERTS, SMOOTHIES AND MORE!

FYI!

COCONUTS HELP TO INCREASE THE QUALITY AND QUANTITY OF ALL SEVEN TISSUES OF THE BODY.

THEY COOL AND STRENGTHEN THE BODY, FILLED WITH SWEETNESS — WE JUST CAN'T GET ENOUGH OF THEM!

"BABA's COCO-MILK"

COCO-NATTY MILK

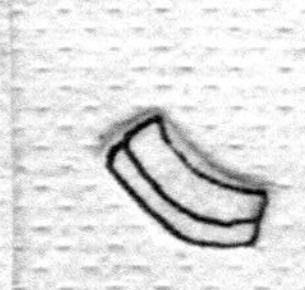

INGREDIENTS

200g MATURE COCONUT FLESH
2 PITTED MEDJOOL DATES
500ML FILTERED WATER.

MAKES 500ML

15 MINUTES

VPKN

ALL YEAR ROUND

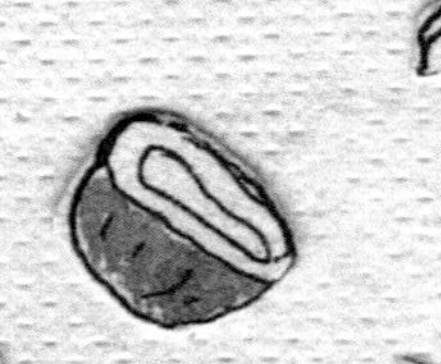

METHOD

1. AFTER CRACKING. OPEN THE COCONUT SHELL, USE A STRONG KNIFE TO CAREFULLY REMOVE THE FLESH. PIT AND DICE THE DATES, MAKING THEMEASIER TO BLEND.

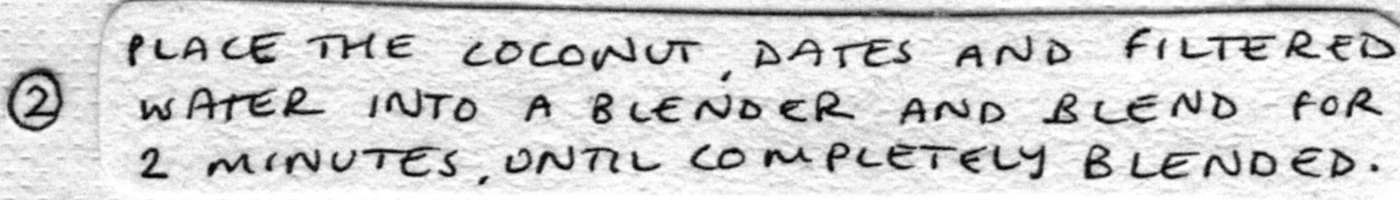

2. PLACE THE COCONUT, DATES AND FILTERED WATER INTO A BLENDER AND BLEND FOR 2 MINUTES, UNTIL COMPLETELY BLENDED.

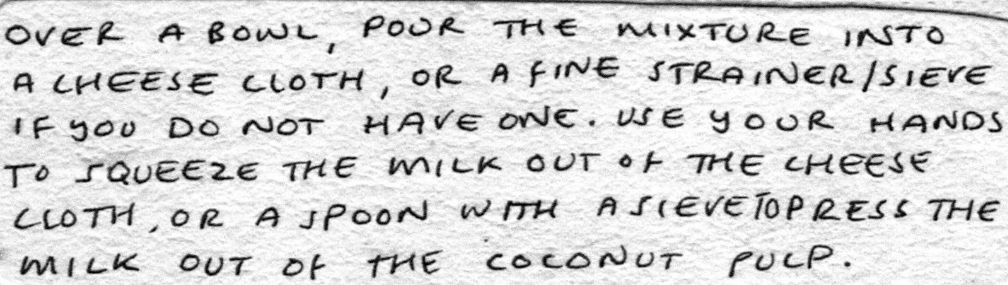

3. OVER A BOWL, POUR THE MIXTURE INTO A CHEESE CLOTH, OR A FINE STRAINER/SIEVE IF YOU DO NOT HAVE ONE. USE YOUR HANDS TO SQUEEZE THE MILK OUT OF THE CHEESE CLOTH, OR A SPOON WITH A SIEVETOPRESS THE MILK OUT OF THE COCONUT PULP.

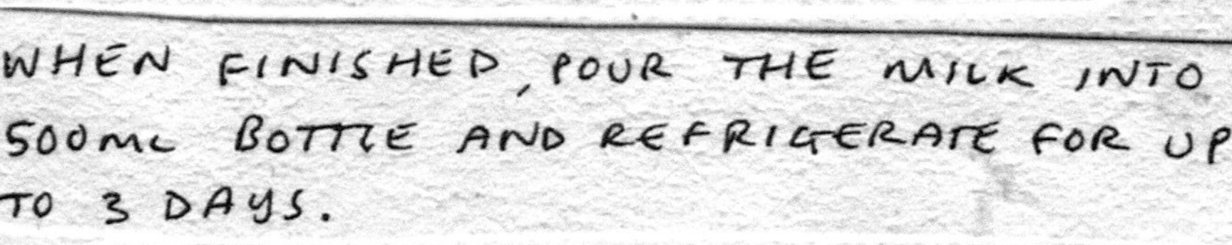

4. WHEN FINISHED, POUR THE MILK INTO A 500ML BOTTLE AND REFRIGERATE FOR UP TO 3 DAYS.

SHAKE SHAKE SHAKE ME!

* YOU CAN REFRIGERATE AND USE THE COCONUT PULP FOR UP TO 3 DAYS AND ADD IT TO CURRIES, GRANOLA, SMOOTHIES, AND MORE!

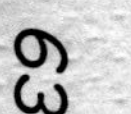

MAKES AROUND 2 x 250ml JARS

VPK~

45 MINUTES

ALL YEAR ROUND

GF V

Date Chutney

INGREDIENTS

750g PITTED MEDJOOL DATES
150g FRESH GINGER (GRATED)
10 SMALL RED CHILLIS
300ML FILTERED WATER
2 TSP CUMIN SEEDS
0.5 TSP GINGER POWDER
2 PINCHES HIMALAYAN SALT.

METHOD

1. PIT THE DATES AND GRATE THE GINGER. USING A LARGE KNIFE, CHOP THE DATES REPEATEDLY UNTIL THEY RESEMBLE A THICK PASTE. TOAST THE CUMIN SEEDS IN A SMALL FRYING PAN FOR 1 MINUTE TO RELEASE THE AROMAS.

2. BOIL THE WATER AND FINELY DICE THE CHILLIS. COMBINE THESE ALONG WITH THE DATES, FRESH GINGER, CUMIN SEEDS, GINGER POWDER AND SALT TO A SMALL POT ON A MEDIUM HEAT.

3. BRING TO BOIL WHILST STIRRING TO COMBINE THE INGREDIENTS AND BREAK UP THE LUMPY DATES. TURN DOWN THE HEAT TO LOW AND COOK FOR AROUND 25 MINUTES, STIRRING OCCASIONALLY TO PREVENT STICKING AND BURNING.

4. THE CHUTNEY SHOULD BE STICKY AND THICK WHEN TIME IS UP. IF IT IS STILL WATERY, CONTINUE COOKING AND STIRRING UNTIL IT RESEMBLES A PASTE.

5. ALLOW THE CHUTNEY TO COOL AND SCOOP IT INTO JARS. KEEP FOR UP TO 2 MONTHS IN THE FRIDGE.

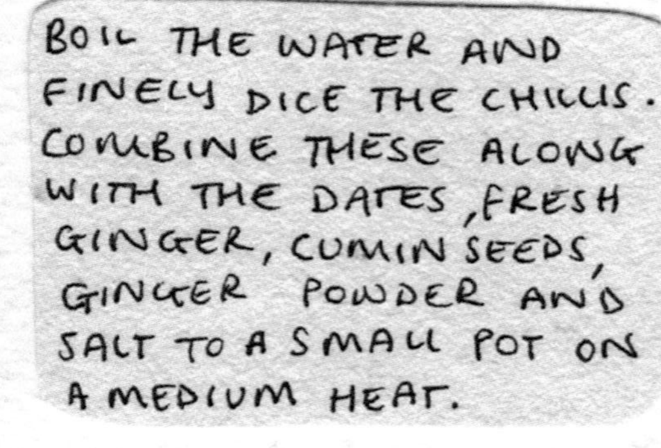

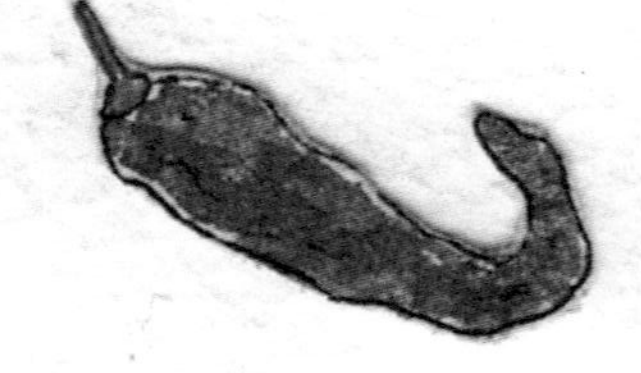

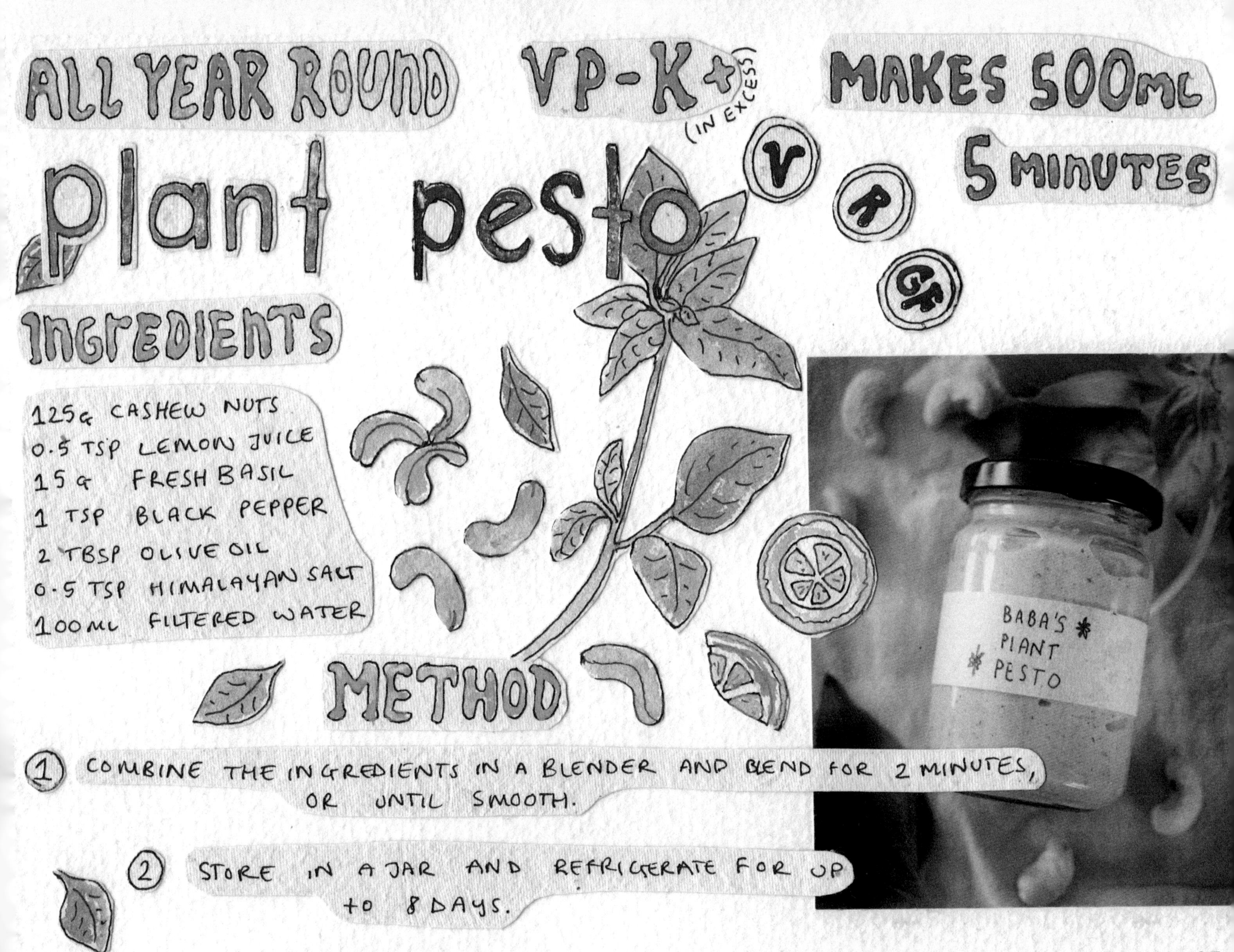
ALL YEAR ROUND
VP-K+ (IN EXCESS)
MAKES 500ML
5 MINUTES
plant pesto
V
R
GF
INGREDIENTS
125G CASHEW NUTS
0.5 TSP LEMON JUICE
15 G FRESH BASIL
1 TSP BLACK PEPPER
2 TBSP OLIVE OIL
0.5 TSP HIMALAYAN SALT
100ML FILTERED WATER
METHOD
1 COMBINE THE INGREDIENTS IN A BLENDER AND BLEND FOR 2 MINUTES, OR UNTIL SMOOTH.
2 STORE IN A JAR AND REFRIGERATE FOR UP TO 8 DAYS.
BABA'S * PLANT * PESTO

MAKES A SMALL JAR | 20 MINUTES | VP-K+ | SUMMER, AUTUMN, EARLY WINTER

BLUEBERRY COMPOTE

(V) (GF)

REFRIGERATE FOR UP TO 2 MONTHS

INGREDIENTS

250g FRESH BLUEBERRIES
0.25 LEMON (JUICE)
50ml FILTERED WATER
3 TBSP ORGANIC COCONUT SUGAR

METHOD

1. HEAT A SMALL POT ON A MEDIUM HEAT AND COMBINE HALF OF THE BLUEBERRIES, LEMON JUICE, WATER AND COCONUT SUGAR. COOK WHILST STIRRING FOR 10 MINUTES.

2. TURN THE HEAT TO LOW-MEDIUM. ADD THE REMAINING BLUEBERRIES AND COOK FOR ANOTHER 8-10 MINUTES.

3. ONCE FINISHED, ALLOW THE COMPOTE TO COOL BEFORE JARRING AND POPPING IT INTO THE REFRIGERATOR OR ON SOME WACKY PANCAKES!

TRY ME WITH... OUR SWEET WONKY PANCAKES

BLUEBERRIES ARE PERFECT FOR SUMMER (PITTA SEASON) AS THEY HAVE REFRIGERANT QUALITIES AND COOL THE BODY DOWN.
FYI!
THEY ARE HIGH IN ANTIOXIDANTS SO HELP THE BODY GET RID OF FREE RADICALS
THEY ALSO REDUCE INFLAMMATION AND TREAT URINARY TRACT INFECTIONS
THE LIST GOES ON AND ON BUT YOU GET THE POINT... EAT YOUR BLUEBERRIES!

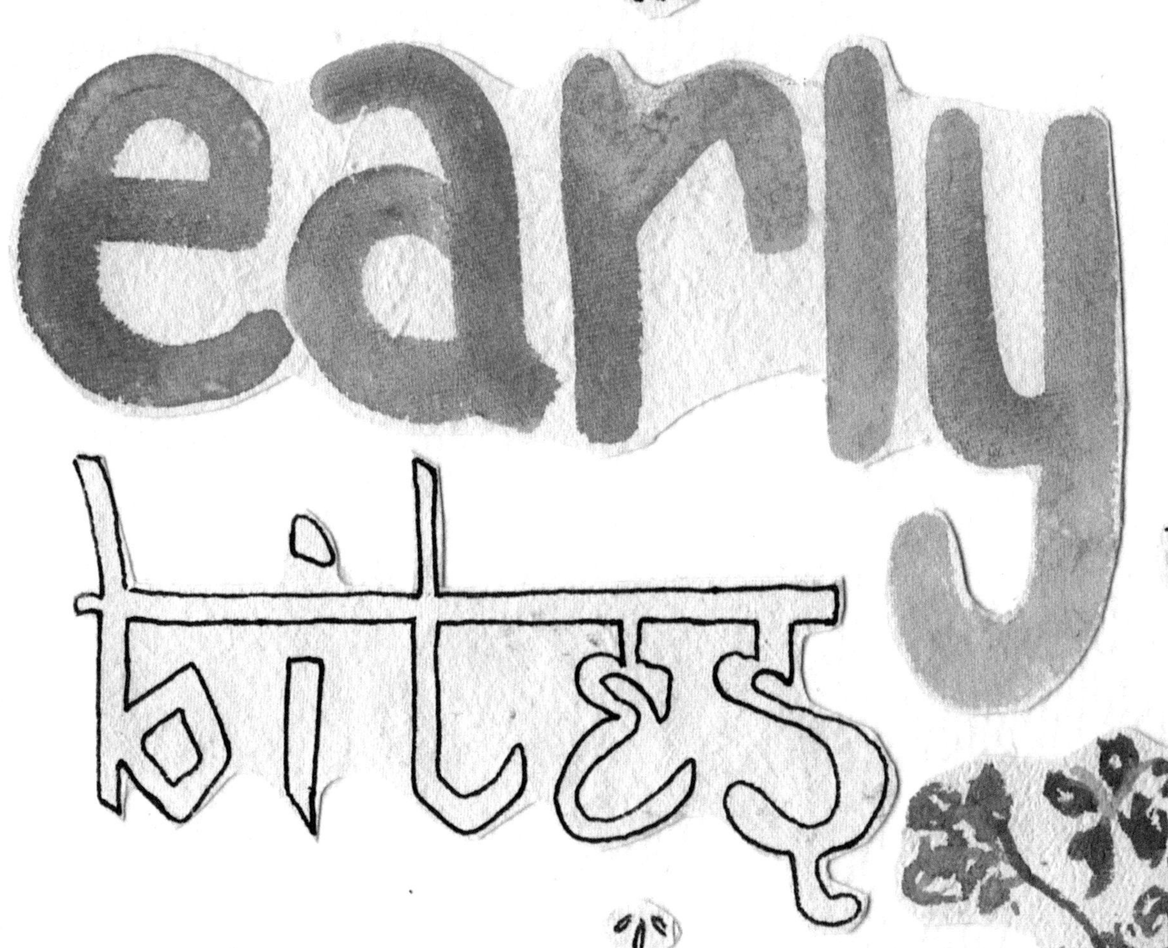

GREEN AVO BOWL

CACAO PARADISE BOWL

BABA'S HERBY BREKKY

THE CLEAN GREEN BREAKFAST MACHINE

GRUNCH GRUNCH GRANOLA

ROOTSY ROAST

WONKY SWEET PANCAKES

WONKY SAVOURY PANCAKES

5 MINUTES

ALL YEAR ROUND

VP-K+

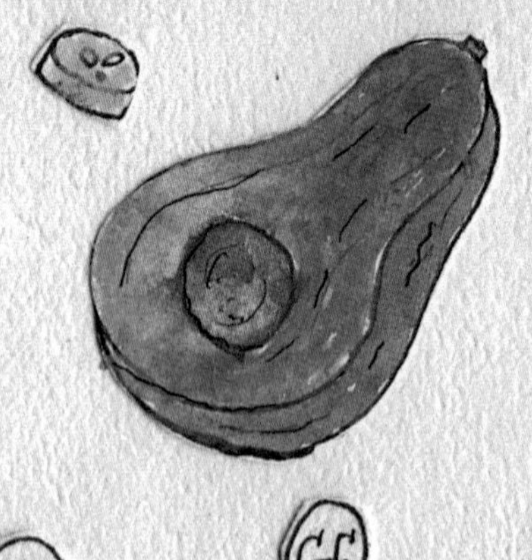

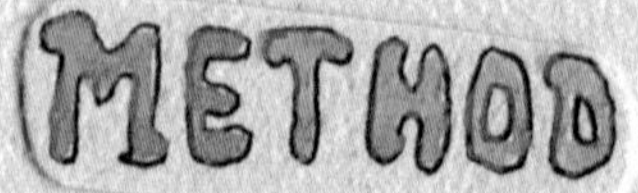

INGREDIENTS

150g	MATURE COCONUT FLESH
250mL	ALMOND MILK
2	BANANAS
1	AVOCADO
1 TSP	SPIRULINA
0.5 TSP	ASHWAGANDHA

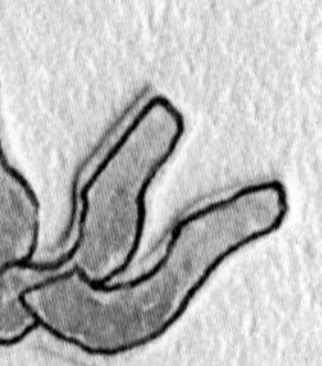

METHOD

1. CAREFULLY REMOVE THE COCONUT FLESH AND THE AVOCADO FROM THEIR SHELLS/SKIN, AND ADD THESE TO A BLENDER ALONG WITH THE ALMOND MILK, BANANAS, SPIRULINA, FENNEL AND ASHWAGANDHA. BLEND FOR 1-2 MINUTES.

2. POUR THE MIX INTO YOUR FAVOURITE BOWL AND TOP WITH YOUR CHOSEN TOPPINGS! IF YOU ARE HUNGRY, WE LIKE TO HAVE A BASE OF DRY OATS TO BE FULLY SATISFIED!

~ ENJOY!! ~

OUR GRUNCH GRUNCH GRANOLA

THIS BOWL IS SUPER GROUNDING AND IS A GREAT BREAKFAST FOR VATA TYPES ESPECIALLY AS IT IS EASY TO DIGEST AND IS NOT TOO COLD FOR THE BODY.

IF YOU LIVE IN THE TROPICS, WE SUGGEST THAT YOU OPT FOR SWEET, TASTY AND LOCAL BANANAS.

THEY ARE OUR GO-TO!

FYI!

WE ARE BANANAS FOR BANANAS!

THEY ARE PACKED WITH ELECTROLYTES THAT KEEP YOU HYDRATED WHEN WATER CAN'T!

VP-K+ (IN EXCESS)

ALL YEAR ROUND

5 MINUTES

SERVES 2

CACAO PARADISE BOWL

(R) (GF) (V)

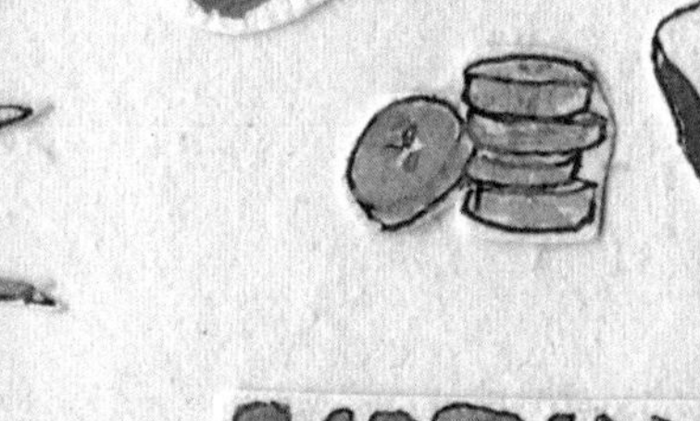

INGREDIENTS

120g	MATURE COCONUT FLESH
2	BANANAS
250ML	ALMOND MILK
2 TBSP	PEANUT BUTTER
1 TBSP	RAW CACAO POWDER
0.5 TSP	GROUND GINGER POWDER

METHOD

1. CAREFULLY REMOVE THE COCONUT FLESH FROM ITS SHELL AND ADD THIS TO A BLENDER ALONG WITH THE BANANAS, ALMOND MILK, PEANUT BUTTER, CACAO POWDER, GINGER POWDER AND BLEND FOR 2 MINUTES!
2. POUR INTO A BOWL AND ENJOY WITH YOUR FAVORITE TOPPINGS!

TRY ME WITH OUR GRUNCH GRUNCH GRANOLA

INGREDIENTS

2 MEDIUM	CARROTS
2 MEDIUM	PARSNIPS
1 LARGE	ZUCCHINI
1 LARGE	BEETROOT
200g	BABY SPINACH <u>OR</u> KALE
0.5	LIME (JUICE)
2 SPRIGS	FRESH ROSEMARY
1 SPRIG	FRESH THYME
7 LEAVES	FRESH OREGANO
7 LEAVES	FRESH BASIL

4 TBSP	OLIVE OIL
400ML	FILTERED WATER (BOILED)
0.5 TSP	GROUND CORIANDER
0.25 TSP	HIMALAYAN SALT.

METHOD

1. CHOP THE CARROTS, PARSNIP, ZUCCHINI AND BEETROOT INTO SHORT 1CM STRIPS. CHOP THE HERBS ROUGHLY. ADD THESE INGREDIENTS TO A MIXING BOWL WITH THE SPINACH, LIME JUICE, OLIVE OIL AND SALT.

   MIX WELL TO COVER THE VEGGIES WITH THE OTHER INGREDIENTS.

2. BOIL THE WATER IN A LARGE POT ON THE STOVE AND REDUCE THE HEAT TO MEDIUM.

3. ADD THE MIXTURE TO A STEAMING BASKET OR LARGE SIEVE AND PLACE THIS OVER THE POT OF BOILING WATER.

4. PLACE THE LID OVER THE MIXTURE AND LET IT STEAM FOR 15 MINUTES, OR UNTIL THE VEG IS COOKED TO YOUR PREFERRED CONSISTENCY!

5. SERVE AS IS OR ALONGSIDE OUR 'SWEETEST BAKED POTATO' RECIPE FOR A FULLER MEAL.

FYI!
HEATING VEGETABLES IN THE OVEN CAN DE-NATURE A LOT OF THE BENEFICIAL ENZYMES, BUT IF YOU STEAM THEM FOR A SHORTER TIME, YOU CAN PREVENT THIS FROM HAPPENING!
PARSNIPS
BEING WARM IN NATURE, PARSNIPS HELP TO PROMOTE SWEATING, MAKING THEM ESPECIALLY GREAT FOR WINTER MEALS.
THEY ARE KAPHA PACIFYING, AS THEY HAVE RAJASIC QUALTIES. THIS HELPS WITH ELIMINATION OF THE BOWELS TOO!

FYI!

WE LOVE STEAMED AND SIMPLE BREAKFASTS!

AS THEY ARE NOT TOO HEAVY TO HAVE IN THE MORNING YOU CAN EASE YOUR DIGESTIVE SYSTEM INTO THE NEW DAY.

35 MINUTES | SERVES 2 | ALL YEAR ROUND

THE CLEAN GREEN BREAKFAST MACHINE

V VPK~ GF

INGREDIENTS

150g	KALE
1	MEDIUM LEEK
1	MEDIUM BROCCOLI
150g	BABY SPINACH
500ML	FILTERED WATER
3 TBSP	TOASTED SESAME OIL <u>OR</u> NORMAL SESAME OIL
1.5 TSP	GROUND CUMIN
1 TSP	BLACK PEPPER
0.5 TSP	HIMALAYAN SALT

METHOD

1. CHOP THE KALE AND LEEK INTO 2CM PIECES AND THE BROCCOLI INTO MEDIUM FLORETS. COMBINE THESE IN A LARGE MIXING BOWL ALONG WITH THE SPINACH, SESAME OIL, CUMIN, BLACK PEPPER AND SALT.

2. BRING THE WATER TO BOIL IN A LARGE POT (ONE THAT CAN REST A LARGE COLANDER INSIDE, WITHOUT TOUCHING THE WATER). TURN THE HEAT TO LOW.

3. USE YOUR CLEAN HANDS TO MASSAGE THE MIX FOR AROUND A MINUTE SO THE KALE BECOMES TENDER AND THE INGREDIENTS ARE WELL COMBINED.

4. PLACE THE INGREDIENTS INTO A LARGE COLANDER AND REST IT INSIDE THE WATER POT. PLACE THE POT'S LID OVER THE VEG-FILLED COLANDER TO STEAM THE VEG FOR 15 MINUTES, OR UNTIL THE BROCCOLI IS COOKED TO YOUR LIKING.

5. SERVE ALONE OR WITH SOME BROWN RICE OR OUR 'SWEETEST-BAKED POTATO' RECIPE. IF YOUR VEG IS ORGANIC, HAVE A DRINK OUT OF THE REMAINING VEG WATER ONCE COOLED!

FYI!
PUMPKIN SEEDS HELP TO
BUILD YOUR BLOOD, WHICH
IMPROVES YOUR ENEGY
AND DIGESTION!
CINNAMON'S WARMING QUALITES
SOOTHE, COMFORT AND CLEAR
OUT THE AIRWAYS.

FILLS x1 1·5L JAR

ALL YEAR ROUND

25 MINUTES

VP∞K+ (IN EXCESS)

INGREDIENTS

100g GF ROLLED OATS
100g BUCKWHEAT FLAKES
100g WALNUTS
70g SUNFLOWER SEEDS
70g FLAKED ALMONDS
50g PUMPKIN SEEDS
40g DESICCATED COCONUT
25g CACAO NIBS
3 TSP CINNAMON
0·25 TSP HIMALAYAN SALT
4-7 TBSP HONEY OR AGAVE NECTAR
70g TURKISH SULTANAS

METHOD

1. PRE-HEAT THE OVEN TO 150°C.

2. CRUSH THE WALNUTS USING THE BACK OF A LARGE KNIFE, WEIGH AND COMBINE ALL THE INGREDIENTS, EXCEPT THE SULTANAS INTO A LARGE MIXING BOWL. ADD THE HONEY OR AGAVE NECTAR TO YOUR DESIRED SWEETNESS.

3. USING CLEAN HANDS, COMBINE THE MIX TOGETHER BY MASSAGING THE INGREDIENTS FOR A FEW MINUTES. MAKE SURE THE STICKINESS OF THE SWEETNER AND OIL IS SPREAD OUT. SQUEEZE LUMPS OF THE GRANOLA TOGETHER TO MAKE IT THICKER.

4. LINE 2 LARGE BAKING TRAYS WITH BAKING PAPER. USE YOUR HANDS TO SQUEEZE THE MIXTURE TOGETHER TO MAKE LARGER CLUMPS (FORMING A FIST WITH YOUR HAND), AND SPREAD THE GRANOLA EVENLY ON THE BAKING PAPER.

5. BAKE FOR 10-13 MINUTES OR UNTIL THE GRANOLA BEGINS TO BROWN/ GOLDEN IN COLOUR. REMOVE FROM THE OVEN WHEN COOKED TO YOUR DESIRED CRUNCHINESS. MIX THE SULTANAS INTO THE GRANOLA AND ALLOW TO COOL BEFORE PLACING INTO JARS.

6. SERVE AS A TOPPING TO YOUR SMOOTHIE BOWLS OR WITH YOUR FAVOURITE PLANT MILK FOR BREKKIE!

ROOTSY

V

SERVES 2

25MIN GF

ROAST

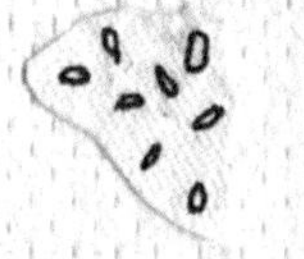

INGREDIENTS

1 LARGE SWEET POTATO
1 SMALL TURNIP
3 MEDIUM CARROTS
1 LARGE LEEK
1 LONG RED BELL PEPPER
2 THUMBS GINGER ROOT
2 SPRIGS FRESH ROSEMARY
2 SPRIGS FRESH THYME.

1.5 TSP TUMERIC ROOT
1 TBSP CORIANDER SEEDS
0.5 TSP CUMIN SEEDS
0.5 TSP CHILLI FLAKES
4 TBSP SESAME OIL

V-PK+

① PRE-HEAT THE OVEN TO 180°C

② CHOP THE SWEET POTATO, TURNIP, CARROTS, LEEK AND BELL PEPPER INTO EQUALLY-SIZED STRIPS; AROUND 0.5 CM THICK.

CHOP THE ROSEMARY AND THYME THEN PEEL AND CHOP THE GINGER INTO THIN STRIPS.

③ ADD THESE INGREDIENTS TO A LARGE MIXING BOWL, ADD THE OIL, SPICES, SALT AND PEPPER. USING A WOODEN SPOON OR YOUR HANDS, MASSAGE THE MIXTURE TOGETHER.

④ LINE 2 BAKING TRAYS WITH BAKING PAPER, THEN EVENLY SPREAD THE MIX OVER THEM. PLACE INTO THE OVEN TO COOK FOR 10-15 MINUTES, CHECKING FOR READINESS.

⑤ REMOVE THE TRAYS FROM THE OVEN WHEN THE VEGGIES BEGIN TO GOLDEN.

⑥ SERVE AND ENJOY!

(V)

INGREDIENTS

* MAKE SURE ALL INGREDIENTS ARE ROOM TEMPERATURE!

0.5 TSP HIMALAYAN SALT
2 TBSP OLIVE OIL
A DASH OF COCONUT OIL TO GREASE THE PAN.
2 TBSP AGAVE NECTAR
1.5 TSP GROUND CINNAMON
2 PINCHES NUTMEG.
2 TBSP 'BLUEBERRY COMPOTE' RECIPE

2 TBSP GROUND FLAXSEED
6 TBSP WARM WATER
300g ORGANIC WHOLEWHEAT FLOUR
500 ML UNSWEETENED ALMOND MILK

FOR TOPPING:
MORE BLUEBERRY COMPOTE!

METHOD

1. IN A MUG, COMBINE THE GROUND FLAXSEED AND WARM WATER. STIR AND LEAVE FOR 3 MINUTES TO MAKE A FLAX-EGG.

2. SIEVE THE WHOLEWHEAT FLOUR INTO A MIXING BOWL, ADD THE FLAX-EGG, ALMOND MILK, SALT AND OLIVE OIL. BEAT THE MIX FOR 2-3 MINUTES UNTIL THE MIXTURE IS SMOOTH. ADD MORE ALMOND MILK FOR THINNER PANCAKES.

3. ADD THE AGAVE NECTAR, CINNAMON, NUTMEG AND BLUEBERRY COMPOTE TO THE MIXTURE, STIRRING FOR ANOTHER MINUTE.

4. ON A MEDIUM-HIGH HEAT, GREASE A 25-30cm FRYING PAN WITH COCONUT OIL USING A PIECE OF KITCHEN ROLL. SPREAD OUT ANY BLOBS OF OIL AS THESE WILL BURN.

5. WHEN THE PAN IS HOT, ADD A LARGE SCOOP (AROUND 0.5 CUPS) OF THE MIX TO THE PAN. FRY FOR AROUND 2 MINUTES ON ONE SIDE. USING A SPATULA TO CURL THE SIDE OF THE PANCAKE TO CHECK IF IT IS BROWNING, AND IF SO FLIP IT. FRY FOR ANOTHER MINUTE OR SO ON THIS SIDE.

* TEST THE FIRST ONE AND COOK FOR A LONGER OR SHORTER TIME DEPENDING HOW YOU LIKE THEM!

6. SERVE WITH MORE BLUEBERRY COMPOTE!

WONKY SWEET PANCAKES

SUMMER, AUTUMN, EARLY WINTER

VP-K+

1 HOUR

MAKES 7-8

WONKY SAVOURY PANCAKES

INGREDIENTS

2 TBSP GROUND FLAXSEED
6 TBSP WARM WATER
300g ORGANIC WHOLEWHEAT FLOUR
500ML UNSWEETENED ALMOND MILK
0.5 TSP HIMALAYAN SALT
2 TBSP OLIVE OIL
A DASH OF COCONUT OIL TO GREASE THE PAN.

1 TSP MUSTARD SEEDS
1 TSP GROUND TUMERIC

FOR THE TOPPING:

1 HANDFUL CHERRY TOMATOES
2 HANDFUL BABY SPINACH
1 TBSP FILTERED WATER
1 TSP OLIVE OIL
A SPRINKLE OF SALT & PEPPER

* MAKE SURE ALL THE INGREDIENTS ARE ROOM TEMPERATURE BEFORE BEGINNING!!

METHOD

1. IN A MUG, COMBINE THE FLAXSEED WITH THE WARM WATER, STIR AND LEAVE FOR 3 MINUTES TO MAKE A FLAX-EGG.

2. SIEVE THE WHOLEWHEAT FLOUR INTO A MIXING BOWL, THEN ADD THE FLAX-EGG, ALMOND MILK, SALT AND OLIVE OIL. BEAT THE MIXTURE FOR 2-3 MINUTES UNTIL THE MIX IS SMOOTH. ADD MORE ALMOND MILK FOR THINNER PANCAKES.

3. ADD THE MUSTARD SEEDS AND GROUND TUMERIC TO THE MIXTURE, STIR FOR ANOTHER MINUTE.

4. ON A MEDIUM-HIGH HEAT, GREASE A 25-30CM FRYING PAN USING COCONUT OIL AND KITCHEN ROLL. REMOVE ALL BLOBS OF OIL AS THESE WILL BURN.

5. WHEN THE PAN IS HOT, ADD A LARGE SCOOP (AROUND 0.5 CUPS) OF THE MIXTURE TO THE PAN. SPREADING IT TO MAKE A PANCAKE SHAPE. FRY FOR 2 MINUTES ON ONE SIDE, USING A SPATULA TO CURL UP THE SIDES TO CHECK FOR BROWNING. FLIP IT OVER AND FRY FOR ANOTHER MINUTE OR SO.

* TEST THE FIRST PANCAKE AND COOK FOR LONGER OR SHORTER DEPENDING ON YOUR PREFERENCE.

6. IN A SEPARATE PAN, COMBINE THE TOMATOES, SPINACH, WATER, OIL AND SALT AND PEPPER AND COOK ON A LOW-MEDIUM HEAT, COVERING FOR 3 MINUTES AND STIRRING OCCASIONALLY.

7. ET VOILA - SERVE ALTOGETHER!

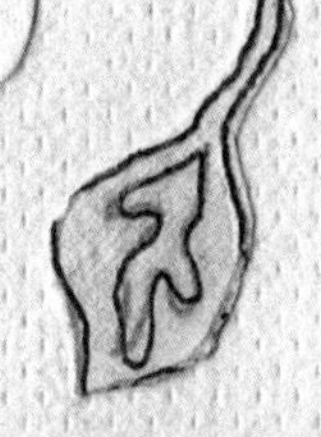

MAKES 7-8 **1 HOUR** **SUMMER, AUTUMN, EARLY WINTER**

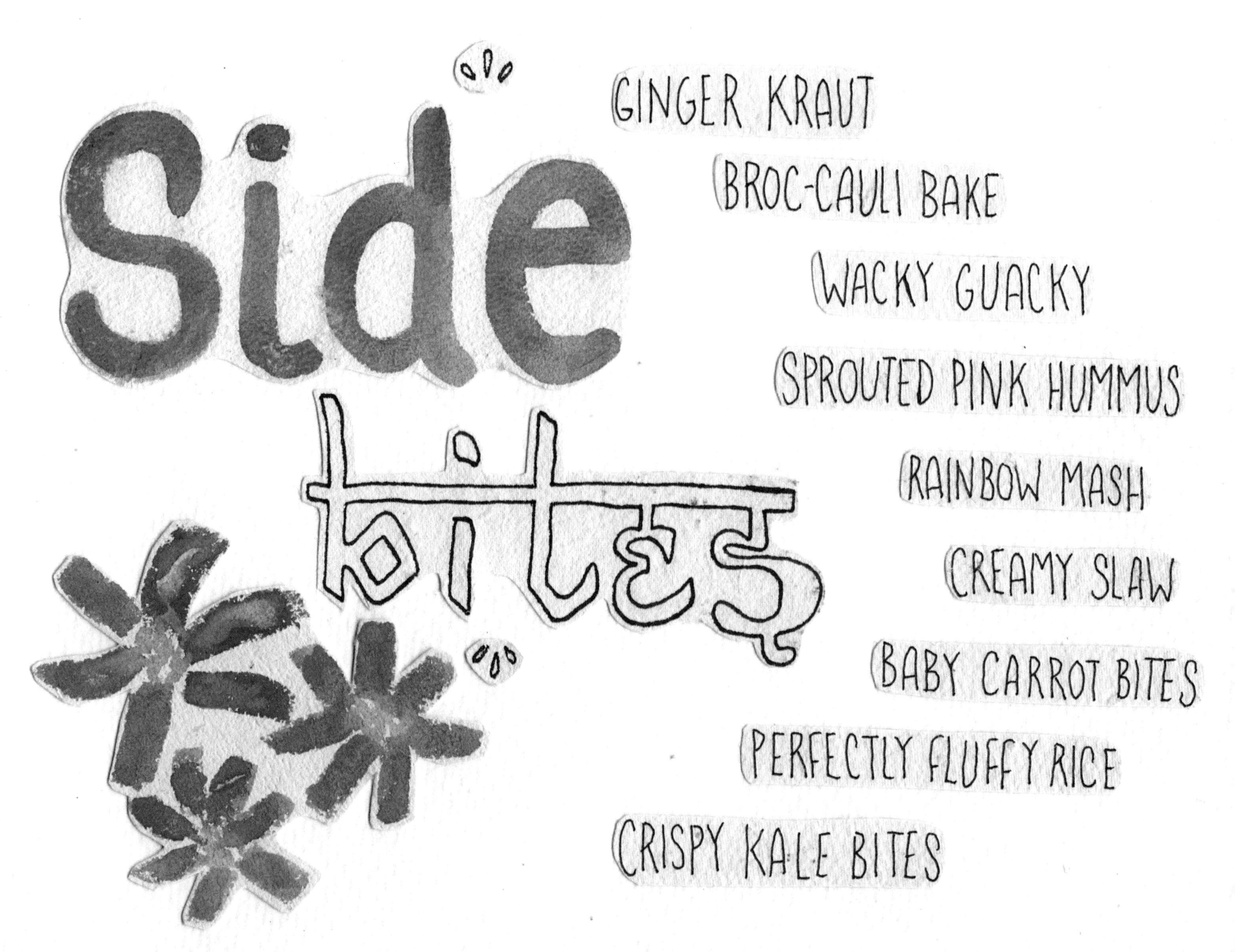
Side bites
GINGER KRAUT
BROC-CAULI BAKE
WACKY GUACKY
SPROUTED PINK HUMMUS
RAINBOW MASH
CREAMY SLAW
BABY CARROT BITES
PERFECTLY FLUFFY RICE
CRISPY KALE BITES

GREAT FOR THE GUT! :)
V
GF
F
ADD YOUR FAVOURITE SPICES OR JUICE ME UP WITH RAW GRATED BEETROOT!
BURP ME TO RELIEVE MY BUBBLINK PRESSURE!
FYI!
*KEEP A WATCHFUL EYE...
THE HOTTER THE ROOM THE QUICKER THE FERMENTATION!

1.5 HOURS

GINGER KRAUT

MAKES 3x 500ML JARS

VP+K-

SPRING & LATE WINTER

INGREDIENTS

1 MEDIUM WHITE CABBAGE
2 MEDIUM CARROTS
4 THUMBS GINGER

1 TSP BLACK PEPPER
4 TSP HIMALAYAN SALT
3 TSP CORIANDER SEEDS
1 TSP CUMIN SEEDS

METHOD

1. STERILISE 3x500ML JARS BY CAREFULLY POURING BOILING WATER OVER THEM.
2. GRATE THE GINGER AND CARROTS, AND SLICE THE CABBAGE INTO THIN, FINE STRIPS BY HAND OR WITH A MANDOLIN. KEEP 4 WHOLE, LARGE LEAVES OF CABBAGE FOR LATER USE.
3. IN ONE OR TWO LARGE BOWLS COMBINE THE SLICED VEGGIES WITH THE SEEDS, SALT AND PEPPER. MASSAGE THE VEG FOR 10 MINUTES UNTIL IT BECOMES WATERY. LEAVE THE MIX TO STAND FOR 1 HOUR.
4. PACK THE MIXTURE INTO THE 3 JARS, PRESSING IT DOWN FIRMLY TO THE BOTTOM OF THE JARS AFTER EACH HANDFUL. LEAVE 5CM OF SPACE AT THE TOP OF JAR.
5. ONCE THE JARS ARE FULL COVER THE MIX WITH THE REMAINING LIQUID.
6. TO KEEP THE MIX PRESSED DOWN, ROLL AND PLACE THE LARGE CABBAGE LEAVES, OR SOMETHING WEIGHTY, ONTO THE MIX AND CLOSE THE JAR.
7. LEAVE FOR 1-4 WEEKS AT ROOM TEMPERATE (27°C), TASTING OCCASIONALLY TO SUIT YOUR LIKING. ONCE READY, PLACE INTO THE FRIDGE AND ENJOY!

FYI!

BROCCOLI AND CAULIFLOWER ARE BOTH GAS-FORMING, SO THIS DISH MAY AGGRIVATE GAS-PRONE VATA TYPES. TO PREVENT THE EXTRA WIND, THESE VEGGIES ARE BEST CURRIED TO AID DIGESTION.

NUTS AND SEEDS ARE BEST EATEN WITH MEALS, LIKE THIS ONE, TO AID THEIR DIGESTION!

BROC-CAULI BAKE

LATE WINTER, SPRING & SUMMER

SERVES 2

25 MINUTES

GF V K

V+ PK-

INGREDIENTS

1 CAULIFLOWER
10 STEMS TENDER STEM BROCCOLI
2 THUMBS GINGER
5 STALKS CAVOLO-NERO KALE.

2 TBSP SESAME OIL
1 TSP SESAME SEEDS
1 TSP PUMPKIN SEEDS
1 TSP SUNFLOWER SEEDS
1 TSP CUMIN SEEDS
1 TSP BLACK PEPPER
0.5 TSP HIMALAYAN SALT.

METHOD

1. PRE-HEAT THE OVEN TO 180°C.
2. CHOP THE CAULIFLOWER INTO FLORETS AND THE ENDS OFF THE BROCCOLI STEMS. PEEL AND GRATE THE GINGER, AND CHOP THE KALE STALKS.
3. IN A LARGE MIXING BOWL COMBINE ALL THE INGREDIENTS WITH THE SESAME OIL AND MIX WELL. ADD A DASH OF WATER TO MAKE THE MIX COMBINE TOGETHER.
4. SPREAD THE MIXTURE EVENLY ON 2 BAKING SHEETS ON THE BAKING TRAYS. DRIZZLE WITH MORE OIL TO YOUR LIKING.
5. PLACE THE TRAYS IN THE OVEN FOR 10-15 MINUTES, CHECKING FOR READINESS THROUGHOUT. REMOVE THE VEG FROM THE OVEN WHEN THE VEG BEGINS TO BROWN. * KEEP AN EYE ON THE KALE, WHICH TENDS TO BURN EASILY.
6. SERVE ALONGSIDE A 'BIG BITE' OR WITH OUR PERFECTLY FLUFFY RICE!

FYI!
AVOCADO IS A DREAM FOOD!
IT IS GROUNDING, BALANCING, FIBROUS, AND ALKALISING, BUT MAKE SURE THEY COME FROM ETHICAL SOURCES!
IF YOUR PITTA IS AGGRAVATED AND YOU HAVE HEARTBURN OR INDIGESTION, THEN AVOCADO IS THE PERFECT FRUIT TO COOL YOU DOWN.

VPK~ ALL YEAR

WACKY GUACKY

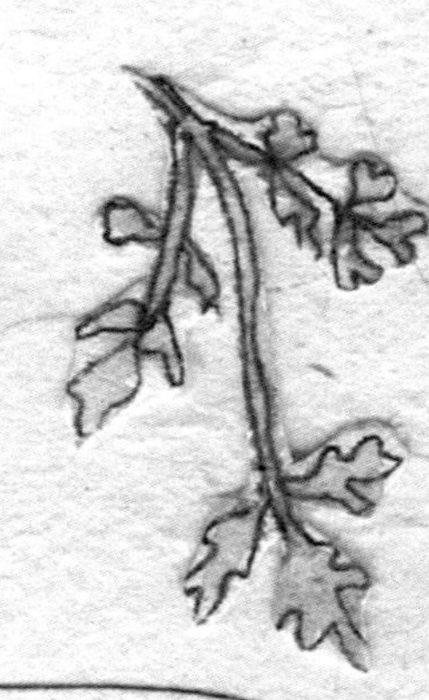

SERVES 4 (AS A SIDE)

V GF K

INGREDIENTS

3 LARGE	RIPE AVOCADOS
0.5 HANDFUL	FRESH CORIANDER
1	LIME (JUICE)
0.5 TSP	NIGELLA SEEDS
1 TSP	CUMIN SEEDS
1 TSP	CORIANDER SEEDS
0.5 TSP	CRUSHED CHILLI
0.25 TSP	HIMALAYAN SALT
0.5 TSP	BLACK PEPPER

METHOD

7 MINUTES

1. CRUSH THE NIGELLA SEEDS, CUMIN AND CORIANDER SEEDS IN A PESTLE AND MORTAR BEFORE ADDING THEM TO A SMALL FRYING PAN. LIGHTLY TOAST FOR 1 MINUTE ON A LOW HEAT TO RELEASE THE FLAVOURS.
2. USE A FORK TO MASH THE PEELED AVOCADOS IN A BOWL AND COMBINE WITH THE CHOPPED FRESH CORIANDER, LIME JUICE, BLACK PEPPER, CRUSHED CHILLIS, SALT AND TOASTED SEEDS.
3. MIX WELL AND ENJOY AS A SIDE BITE OR MIX INTO OUR 'QUINOA BOWL' RECIPE.

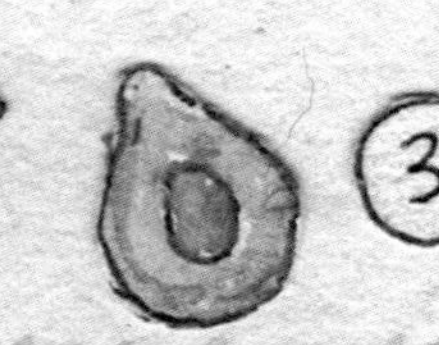

MOST LEMONS ARE WAXED WITH INEDIBLE CHEMICALS TO PREVENT THEM FROM GOING OFF. IT IS MUCH BETTER TO BUY YOUR LEMONS FRESH AND OPT FOR ORGANIC, UNWAXED ONES.

THIS RECIPE NEEDS A WHOLE LEMON TO BE USED, INCLUDING THE RIND, SO DON'T GO ACCIDENTALLY ADDING NASTY CHEMICALS TO YOUR FOOD WITHOUT KNOWING IT!

FYI!

THE FIBRE IN CHICKPEAS IS NEARLY 75% INSOLUBLE - WHICH MEANS THEY ARE GREAT FOR BULKING UP YOUR STOOLS :)

PINK SPROUTED hummus

INGREDIENTS

4 TBSP OLIVE OIL
4 TBSP TAHINI
1 TSP CUMIN SEEDS
0.5 TSP BLACK PEPPER
0.5 TSP HIMALAYAN SALT
0.5 LEMON (UNWAXED!!)
1.5 THUMBS GINGER
0.5 MEDIUM BEETROOT
1 MEDIUM RED HOT CHILLI
315 g SPROUTED CHICKPEAS (USING THE 'SPROUTED ALMOST ANYTHING' RECIPE)

MAKES x1

250 ML JAR

30 MINUTES

ALL YEAR ROUND

VKPN

METHOD

1

IN A BLENDER OR FOOD PROCESSOR COMBINE THE FULL LEMON; IN CHUNKS WITH SKIN ON, THE PEELED AND GRATED GINGER, OLIVE OIL AND TAHINI. BLEND FOR 2 MINUTES OR UNTIL ANY BIG LUMPS HAVE GONE. YOU MAY NEED TO USE A WOODEN SPOON TO STIR THE MIXTURE INTERMITTENTLY.

2

IN A SMALL FRYING PAN, TOAST THE CUMIN SEEDS FOR 2 MINUTES TO RELEASE THE AROMAS AND ADD THESE TO THE BLENDER.

3

PEEL AND CHOP THE BEETROOT INTO SMALL PIECES AND ADD THESE TO THE BLENDER AS WELL WITH THE PEPPER, SALT, CHOPPED CHILLI AND SPROUTED CHICKPEAS.
BLEND FOR ANOTHER 3-4 MINUTES, STIRRING AGAIN, IF NEEDED. ADD A DASH OF WATER IF THE MIXTURE IS TOO THICK.

4

WHEN FINISHED SPOON THE HUMMUS INTO YOUR JAR OF CHOICE, CHILL AND ENJOY WITHIN 2-3 DAYS.

VPK ~ ALL YEAR ROUND

30 MINUTES SERVES 4

Rainbow Mash

GF

V

INGREDIENTS

- 4 SWEET POTATOES (MIX OF PURPLE, YELLOW, AND ORANGE).
- 4 SPRIGS FRESH ROSEMARY
- 0.5 HANDFUL FRESH PARSLEY
- 1 L FILTERED WATER
- 4 TBSP OLIVE OIL
- 1 TSP HIMALAYAN SALT
- 1 TSP CUMIN SEEDS

METHOD

1. PEEL AND CHOP THE SWEET POTATOES INTO 2CM CUBES. ADD THEM TO A POT WITH ENOUGH BOILED WATER TO COVER THEM.
   BRING TO A BOIL ON A MEDIUM-HEAT AND LEAVE TO COOK FOR 20 MINUTES OR UNTIL THE POTATOES ARE SOFT ENOUGH TO EFFORTLESSLY PIERCE WITH A FORK.

2. REMOVE THE ROSEMARY FROM THEIR STEMS AND LIGHTLY TOAST THEM WITH THE CUMIN SEEDS IN A SMALL FRYING PAN FOR 2 MINUTES TO RELEASE THEIR AROMAS.

3. STRAIN THE WATER, KEEPING AROUND 50ML WITH THE POTATOES. MASH THE POTATOES WITH THE OLIVE OIL, SALT, CUMIN SEEDS AND ROSEMARY, AND CHOPPED PARSLEY.
   ADD MORE WATER IF YOU LIKE YOUR MASH CREAMIER.

GOOD FOR ALL BODY TYPES, THE FIBRE IN THESE SWEET TATTIES ASSISTS WITH SMOOTH DIGESTION.

FYI!

SWEET POTATOES ARE SPLEEN TONICS AND HELP WITH THE PRODUCTION OF BLOOD. THEY ALSO BUILD AGNI, YOUR DIGESTIVE FIRE, BRIGHTENING YOUR APPEARANCE AND PROVIDING A FEELING OF STABILITY, — ESPECIALLY FOR VATA TYPES.

FYI!
THIS AWESOME PLANT-BASED CASHEW COLESLAW DISH IS A GREAT SPIN ON THE ORIGINAL - CREAMINESS WITHOUT THE CRUELTY.
WE ADD CARAWAY SEEDS TO LESSEN THE WIND-CAUSING EFFECTS OF THE RAW VEGGIES.

CREAMY SLAW

35 MINUTES

SERVES 6

SPRING, SUMMER

V+ PK-

INGREDIENTS

3 MEDIUM CARROTS
0·25 RED CABBAGE
0·25 WHITE CABBAGE
0·5 HANDFUL FRESH PARSLEY

DRESSING:
2 THUMBS GINGER
0·5 LEMON (JUICE)
200g CASHEWS (UNSALTED)
150mL FILTERED WATER
1 TSP CARAWAY SEEDS
1 TSP BLACK PEPPER
0·25 TSP HIMALAYAN SALT (OPTIONAL)

METHOD

*FOR BEST RESULTS, SOAK THE CASHEWS FOR 1 HOUR IN HOT WATER BEFORE STARTING.

1. USING EITER A MANDOLIN WITH THE COASE BLADE OR A NORMAL GRATER, SHED THE TWO QUARTERS OF CABBAGE AND CARROTS. CHOP THE PARSLEY FINELY, AND ADD THESE TO A LARGE MIXING BOWL.
2. CHOP THE GINGER INTO SMALL CHUNKS AND COMBINE WITH THE LEMON JUICE, CASHEWS, WATER, CARAWAY SEEDS, BLACK PEPPER AND SALT INTO A FOOD-PROCESSOR OR BLENDER FOR 2 MINUTES OR UNTIL SMOOTH.
3. ADD THE BLENDED MIX TO THE MIXING BOWL AND STIR IT IN WELL SO THAT THE SHREDDED VEG IS COATED.
4. SERVE GARNISHED WITH MORE PARSLEY AND ENJOY!

25 MINUTES SERVES 2 ALL YEAR ROUND VPK

baby carrot bites

GF V K

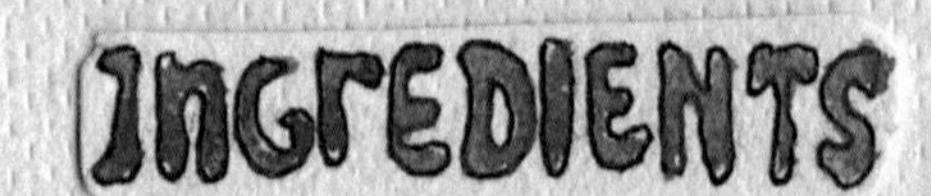

- 2 THUMBS FRESH GINGER
- 25 BABY MIXED-COLOURED CARROTS
- 3 SPRIGS FRESH ROSEMARY
- 1 TBSP SESAME OIL
- 2 TBSP BLACK SESAME SEEDS
- 2 TBSP ORGANIC TAHINI.

METHOD

1. PRE HEAT THE OVEN TO 180°c
2. CHOP THE GINGER INTO THIN STRIPS AND CHOP THE ROSEMARY. ADD THESE TO A LARGE MIXING BOWL WITH THE CARROTS, SESAME OIL AND SESAME SEEDS. MIX WELL!
3. LINE A BAKING TRAY WITH BAKING PAPER AND SPREAD THE MIX OUT ON THE PAPER BEFORE PLACING IT INTO THE OVEN. BAKE FOR 20 MINUTES OR UNTIL THE CARROTS ARE COOKED TO YOUR PREFERRED CONSISTENCY.
4. DRIZZLE WITH TAHINI TO SERVE AND ENJOY!

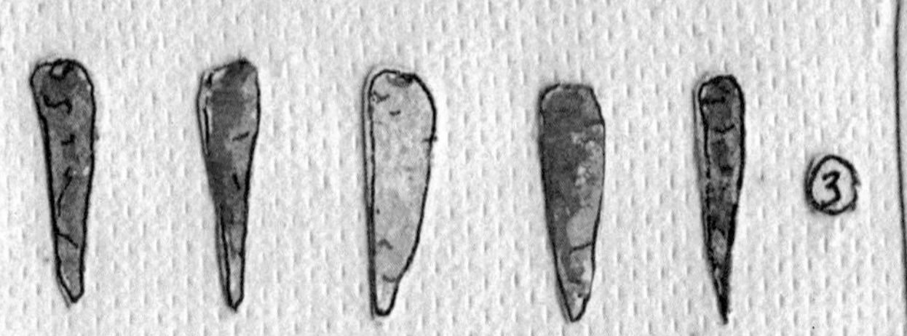

FYI!
LABELLED 'TINY GINSENG' - CARROTS ARE HIGHLY ALKALISING AND INCREASE BOTH 'PRANA' (LIFE FORCE ENERGY) AND 'OJAS' (VITALITY).

ENJOY ME
WITH MANY
BIG BITES!
FYI!
BASMATI RICE IS HIGHLY NOURISHING AND EASY TO
DIGEST WHEN EATEN IN MODERATION.
IT IS A GREAT SOURCE OF PRANA (LIFE FORCE ENERGY)
AND WILL HELP YOUR BODY BUILD BODILY TISSUES.

PERFECTLY FLUFFY RICE

V GF

INGREDIENTS

200ML ORGANIC COCONUT MILK.
1 SPRIG FRESH CORIANDER
~2L FILTERED WATER.

3 CUPS (600g) ORGANIC WHITE BASMATI RICE (UNCOOKED)
1 TSP HIMALAYAN SALT
1 TSP CUMIN POWDER
1 TSP MUSTARD SEEDS

SUMMER, AUTUMN, EARLY WINTER

VP-K+

SERVES 4

30MIN

METHOD

1. WASH AND DRAIN THE UNCOOKED RICE AND ADD THIS TO A MEDIUM SIZED PAN ALONG WITH THE SALT, CUMIN AND MUSTARD SEEDS.
2. ADD COCONUT MILK TO THE PAN. BOIL THE KETTLE WITH 800ML OF FILTERED WATER. POUR ENOUGH WATER OVER THE RICE TO COVER WITH 1.5CM ABOVE OF WATER. BRING TO BOIL ON A HIGH HEAT STIRRING FREQUENTLY TO PREVENT THE RICE FROM STICKING TO THE PAN, FOR 8 MINUTES, OR UNTIL ALL THE LIQUID IS ABSORBED.
3. DRAIN THE RICE INTO A SIEVE OR COLANDER. FILL THE NOW EMPTY PAN WITH ANOTHER 800ML OF WATER AND HEAT THIS ON A LOW-MEDIUM HEAT ON THE STOVE. PLACE THE SIEVE OR COLANDER OVER THE PAN RIM AND COVER THE RICE WITH A PAN-LID TO STEAM THE RICE FOR ANOTHER 15-20 MINUTES, OR UNTIL THE RICE IS YOUR PREFERRED CONSISTENCY.
4. ONCE FINISHED, POUR THE RICE INTO A BOWL, FLUFFING IT WITH A FORK AND GARNISHING WITH FRESH CORIANDER.

FYI!

WE USE PINK HIMALAYAN SALT IN OUR RECIPES, WHICH CONTAINS UP TO 84 TRACE MINERALS AND ELEMENTS (WHICH WE NEED FOR OPTIMUM BODY FUNCTION) UNLIKE TABLE SALT, WHICH ONLY CONTAINS TWO — SODIUM + CHLORIDE.

KALE HAS A STIMULATING BITTERNESS THAT HELPS TO JUMP-START YOUR CIRCULATION AND GET THE BLOOD FLOWING. KALE CAN, HOWEVER, AGGRAVATE VATA IN EXCESS DUE TO ITS DRY NATURE.

CRISPY KALE BITES

SPRING + SUMMER

VPK+
(IN EXCESS)

SERVES 2-4

25 MINUTES

INGREDIENTS

- 200 g KALE (CAVOLO NERO)
- 4 TBSP OLIVE OIL
- 0.5 TSP GINGER POWDER
- 0.5 TSP PAPRIKA POWDER
- 0.5 TSP BLACK PEPPER
- 0.25 TSP CAYENNE PEPPER
- 0.25 TSP HIMALAYAN SALT

+ OPTIONAL TAHINI!

(V) (GF)

METHOD

1. PRE-HEAT THE OVEN TO 160°C
2. CHOP THE KALE INTO 2CM-WIDTH PIECES, AND COMBINE IT ALONG WITH THE REMAINING INGREDIENTS INTO A MIXING BOWL. MASSAGE WITH YOUR HANDS TO COAT THE KALE WITH THE SPICES AND OIL.
3. SPREAD OUT EVENLY ON A BAKING TRAY LINED WITH BAKING PAPER, (YOU MAY NEED TWO) AND POP IN THE OVEN. BAKE FOR 15-20 MINUTES, DEPENDING ON YOUR PREFERRED CRISPINESS. CHECK EVERY 5 MINUTES FOR BURNING. THEY SHOULD JUST BE TURNING CRISPY WHEN YOU REMOVE THEM FROM THE OVEN.
4. SERVE AND ENJOY WITH A DRIZZLE OF TAHINI!

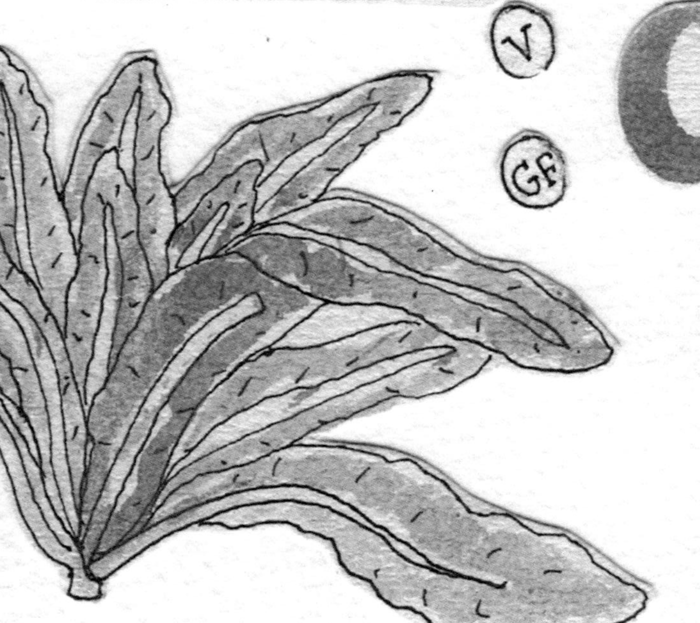

Light
bites
QUINOA BOWL
COCO-LEEK BAKE
BUTTER-NUTTY NOODLES
THE SWEETEST BAKED POTATO
ZUCCHINI PESTO PASTA
RASPA MELLOWMAN SALAD
BALSAMIC KALETTES
THE ORIGINAL STIR-FRY
NO FAFF-FALAFFIES
+TAHINI DRESSING

SERVES 4
30 MINUTES
V
GF
INGREDIENTS
300g QUINOA
500ML FILTERED WATER
150g BABY SPINACH
2 TBSP SESAME OIL
1 BROCCOLI
2 LONG RED PEPPERS
2 CARROTS
1.5 TSP PAPRIKA
0.5 TSP SALT
1 TSP PEPPER
1 LARGE HANDFUL FRESH CORIANDER
200g 'WACKY GUACKY' RECIPE.
+ MORE SESAME OIL TO DRIZZLE.
quinoa
BOWL

METHOD

1. PLACE THE DRY QUINOA INTO A POT AND COVER IT WITH WATER. BRING TO BOIL AND COOK ON LOW-MEDIUM HEAT FOR 20MINUTES. STIRRING OCCASSIONALLY AND ADDING MORE WATER WHEN NEEDED. THE QUINOA SHOULD BE DRY YET SOFT WHEN READY.

2. MEANWHILE, CHOP THE BROCCOLI INTO SMALL FLORRETS, RED PEPPER WIDTH-WAYS AND CARROTS INTO THIN CIRCLES. CHOP THE CORIANDER FINELY.

3. IN A SKILLET, HEAT THE SESAME OIL WITH 2TBSP OF WATER ON A LOW HEAT. ADD THE CHOPPED VEGGIES, PAPRIKA, PEPPER AND SALT. LEAVE THE CORIANDER TO ONE SIDE FOR LATER USE. COVER THE SKILLET WITH A LID AND LEAVE THE VEGGIES TO STEAM FOR 10 MINUTES, STIRRING OCCASIONALLY.

4. WHEN THE VEG IS COOKED TO YOUR LIKING, ADD THE COOKED QUINOA TO THE SKILLET, MIXING IT INTO THE VEGGIES. ADD MORE SESAME OIL IF NEEDED. LEAVE TO COOL WITH THE HEAT OFF FOR 5 MINUTES.

5. POUR THE MIXTURE INTO A SALAD BOWL OF SPINACH. ADD THE WACKY GUACKY MIXTURE AND FRESH CORIANDER. STIR WELL TO COVER ALL THE MIX WITH AVOCADO.

6. SERVE AS A SIDE BITE OR A SIMPLE LIGHT BIG BITE!

V+ PK-

LATE WINTER
SPRING &
SUMMER

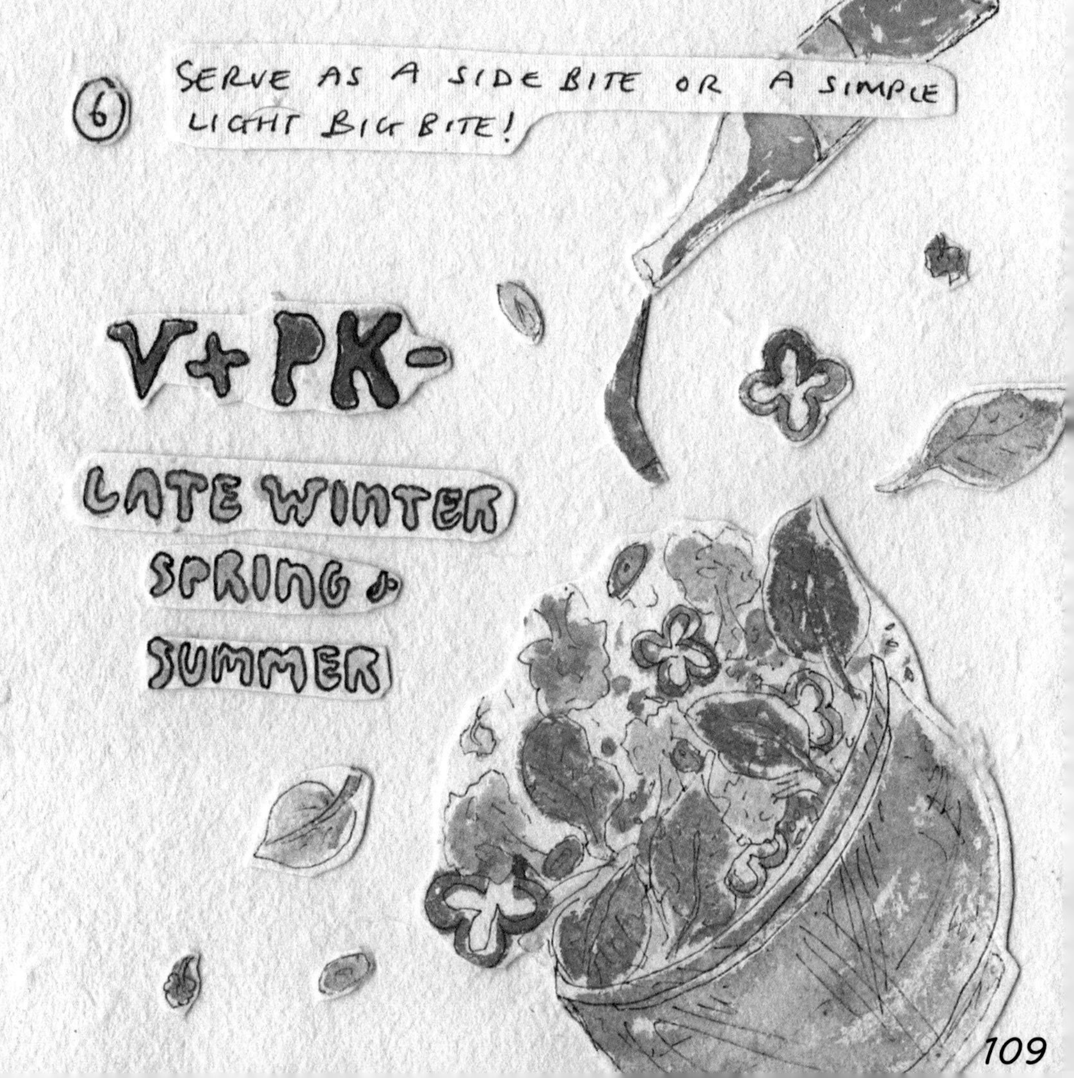

INGREDIENTS

0.75 MATURE COCONUT FLESH
2 MEDIUM LEEKS
3 SPRIGS FRESH ROSEMARY
1.5 TBSP COCONUT OIL
0.75 TSP CAYENNE PEPPER
0.5 TSP BLACK PEPPER
0.25 TSP HIMALAYAN SALT

METHOD

1. PREHEAT THE OVEN TO 180°C. BEGIN BY CHOPPING THE COCONUT FLESH INTO THIN STRIPS AND THE LEEK INTO 1.5cm CHUNKS. CHOP THE ROSEMARY ROUGHLY.
2. MIX THE LEEK, COCONUT, ROSEMARY, CAYENNE PEPPER, BLACK PEPPER AND SALT TOGETHER IN A LARGE MIXING BOWL.
3. LINE A BAKING TRAY WITH BAKING PAPER AND SPREAD THE MIXTURE OUT EVENLY ONTO IT. POP THE TRAY INTO THE OVEN FOR 12-15 MINUTES, USING A SPATULA TO TURN OVER THE VEG AT AROUND 10 MINUTES OF COOKING.
4. SERVE ALONGSIDE BROWN RICE AND AVOCADO FOR A FULL, BALANCING MEAL!

FYI!
IF YOUR COCONUT TENDS TO BE SOLID IN YOUR COOLER CLIMATE, MIX IT WITH SOME HOT WATER BEFORE USING IT TO COOK.
LEEKS CONTAIN ALLYL-SULFIDES, WHICH CAN HELP TO SUPPRESS TUMOUR GROWTH AND PROVIDE PROTECTION FOR THE LININGS IN THE BLOOD VESSELS AGAINST ANY NASTY FREE RADICALS!
WE USE LEEKS INSTEAD OF ONIONS IN SOME OF OUR DISHES AS THEY TEND TO BE MORE 'SATTVIC' IN NATURE.

THIS - ALMOST RAW-DISH IS ONE OF OUR FAVOURITES!
JUST THROW IT ALL TOGETHER IN 30 MINUTES AND ENJOY IT IN THE SUNSHINE.
FYI!
FEEL FREE TO ADD MORE SESAME SEEDS - THEY ARE A MAGICAL FOOD THAT HELP WITH ALL THINGS FROM REPRODUCTIVE HEALTH TO SLEEP, SKIN CARE AND BONE STRENGTH.
THEY MAY BE SMALL, BUT THEY ARE MIGHTY!

SERVES 2 VPK~ ALL YEAR

INGREDIENTS

2 TBSP COCONUT OIL
1 BUTTERNUT SQUASH
75 G SPROUTED MUNG BEANS
1 TSP SESAME SEEDS

AVOCADO SAUCE

2 AVOCADOS
0.5 HANDFUL FRESH PARSLEY
1 TSP GROUND CORIANDER SEEDS
1 LIME JUICE
0.5 TSP HIMALAYAN SALT
50 ML FILTERED WATER

METHOD

1. PEEL AND CUT THE SQUASH LENGTHWAYS AND REMOVE THE SEEDS. USING A MANDOLIN WITH A THICK BLADE OR A WIDE VEGETABLE HAND PEELER, SLICE THE SQUASH LENGTHWAYS ALONG THE BLADE TO MAKE LONG STRIPS.

2. HEAT THE COCONUT OIL IN A LARGE SKILLET ON A LOW-MEDIUM HEAT, ADD THE SLICED SQUASH. COOK FOR 7-12 MINS (DEPENDING ON THE THICKNESS OF THE SQUASH). COVER WITH A LID, STIRRING FREQUENTY TO STOP STICKING TO SKILLET.

3. MEANWHILE, USE A PESTLE AND MORTAR TO GRIND THE CORIANDER SEEDS.

   ADD THIS TO A BLENDER ALONG WITH THE AVOCADO, CHOPPED PARSLEY, LIME JUICE, SALT AND WATER.

   BLEND FOR 2 MINUTES OR UNTIL THE MIXTURE IS BLENDED TO YOUR DESIRED CONSISTENCY.

4. REMOVE THE SKILLET FROM THE HEAT AND STIR-IN THE AVOCADO SAUCE AND SPROUTED MUNG BEANS (OR ANY OTHER SPROUTS YOU FANCY!)

   SPRINKLE WITH SESAME SEEDS AND ENJOY!

SERVES 1 | 1 HOUR | VPK~ | ALL YEAR ROUND

The sweetest (BAKED) potato

INGREDIENTS

- 1 MEDIUM SWEET POTATO
- 1 TBSP COCONUT OIL
- 0.5 TSP CUMIN POWDER
- 2 PINCHES HIMALAYAN SALT
- 2 PINCHES BLACK PEPPER

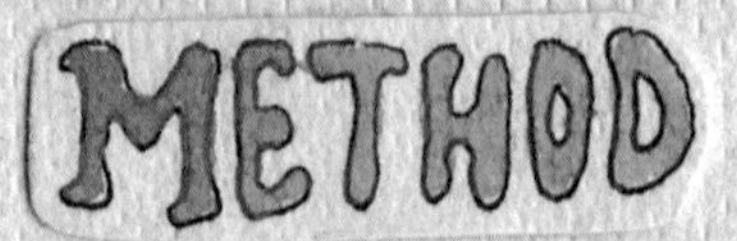

1. PRE-HEAT THE OVEN TO 210°C

2. PREPARE A BAKING TRAY WITH BAKING PAPER. WASH AND SCRUB THE SWEET POTATO SKIN & USING A FORK, PIERCE THE POTATO 8 TIMES.

3. IN A LITTLE MIXING BOWL, MIX THE COCONUT OIL (IF SOLID, HEAT THE OIL GENTLY BEFORE USING IT), CUMIN POWDER, SALT AND PEPPER. USING A BRUSH, COAT THE SWEET POTATO WITH THIS MIXTURE AND PLACE IT ON THE BAKING TRAY.

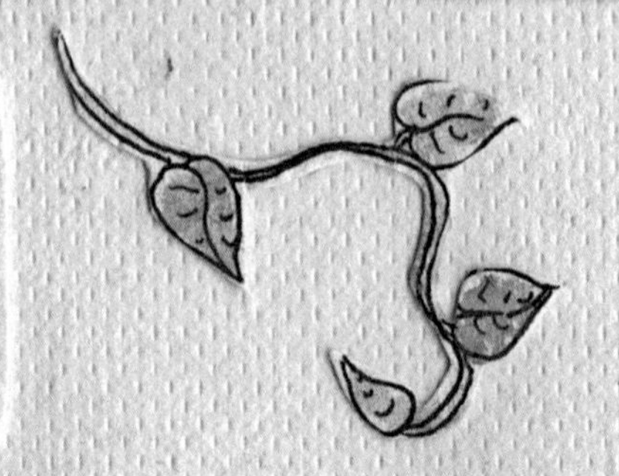

4. WHEN THE OVEN IS HOT ENOUGH, POP THE TRAY INTO THE OVEN AND BAKE FOR 40 MINUTES – 1 HOUR, DEPENDING ON THE SIZE OF THE POTATO. CHECK THE POTATO AT 40 MINUTES BY STICKING A FORK INTO IT. WHEN READY, THE FORK SHOULD PIERCE THE CENTRE WITH NO RESISTANCE.

5. GARNISH WITH ANYTHING YOU FANCY – OUR FAVORITES ARE THE 'WACKY-GUACKY' AND 'CLEAN GREEN BREAKFAST MACHINE'!

FYI!
SWEET POTATOES ARE RICH IN COMPLEX CARBOHYDRATES, WHICH MEANS THAT THESE ROOTS CAN SATISFY THE APPETITE FOR LONG PERIODS OF TIME.
THEY ARE ALSO GREAT FOR DIABETICS — DESPITE THEIR NAME.
WRAPPING THE POTATOES IN FOIL TENDS TO MAKE THE SKIN WET AND SOFT —
BAKING THEM BARE MAKES FOR A MUCH BETTER (AND CRISPIER) MEAL!

FYI!
RAW FOOD IS AN IMPORTANT PART OF A BALANCED DIET.
COOKING FOOD CAN LOWER IT'S VIBRATIONAL FREQUENCY AND DEPLETE THEIR ESSENTIAL NUTRIENTS AND ENZYMES.
WARNING
THE SPRING ONIONS MAY BE A LITTLE OVER-POWERING WHEN SERVED RAW, SO TEST ONE FIRST.

Zucchini pesto pasta

GF

R

V

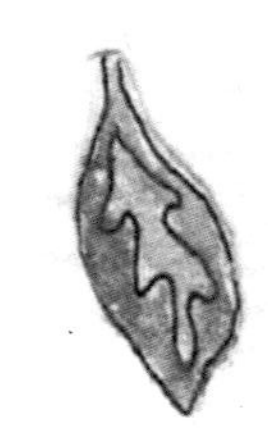

LATE WINTER

SPRING

SUMMER

V+ PK-

SERVES 2

25 MINUTES

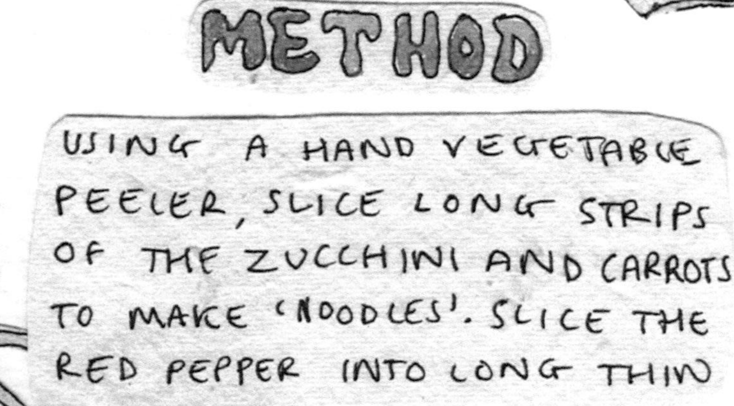

INGREDIENTS

- 2 MEDIUM ZUCCHINIS
- 2 MEDIUM CARROTS
- 1 MEDIUM RED BELL PEPPER
- 130G BABY SPINACH
- 500ML 'PLANT PESTO' RECIPE
- 2 TSP SESAME SEEDS
- 1 SPRING ONION (OPTIONAL)

METHOD

1. USING A HAND VEGETABLE PEELER, SLICE LONG STRIPS OF THE ZUCCHINI AND CARROTS TO MAKE 'NOODLES'. SLICE THE RED PEPPER INTO LONG THIN STRIPS.
2. ADD THE PREPARED VEG, ALONG WITH THE SPINACH AND 'PLANT PESTO' RECIPE TO A MIXING BOWL AND MIX WELL.
3. SERVE WITH A GARNISH OF SESAME SEEDS AND SPRING ONION.

MELLOWMAN SALAD

20 MINUTES | SERVES 2 | V+PK-

LATE WINTER, SPRING, SUMMER

INGREDIENTS

0.5 TSP CUMIN SEEDS
3 TBSP SESAME OIL
2 TBSP SESAME SEEDS
2 TBSP ORGANIC BALSAMIC VINEGAR
0.25 TSP HIMALAYAN SALT

1 LONG RED PEPPER
10 CHERRY TOMATOES
1 SMALL BEETROOT
0.5 CUCUMBER
150g BABY SPINACH
0.5 HANDFUL FRESH CORIANDER
80g SPROUTED CHICKPEAS
60g SPROUTED MUNGBEANS
40g SPROUTED ADZUKI BEANS
100g ORGANIC TEMPEH (OPTIONAL)

METHOD

1. USE THE 'SPROUTING (ALMOST) ANYTHING' RECIPE TO SPROUT THE CHICKPEAS, MUNG-BEANS AND ADZUKI BEANS FOR 1-2 DAYS.
2. CHOP THE TEMPEH INTO 3cm x 0.5cm PIECES. HEAT A SMALL FRYING PAN ON A LOW HEAT AND ADD THE TEMPEH. DRY-FRY THE TEMPEH FOR 4 MINUTES, TOSSING IT TO COOK EVENLY. ADD THE CUMIN SEEDS FOR AN EXTRA MINUTE AND TURN OFF THE HEAT. WHEN FINISHED, ADD THESE TO A MIXING BOWL.
3. CHOP THE LONG RED PEPPER INTO 0.5 cm STRIPS, CHOP THE CHERRY TOMATOES IN HALF, PEEL AND GRATE THE BEETROOT. CHOP THE CUCUMBER IN HALF LENGTH-WAYS AND SLICE THE TWO-HALVES INTO THIN SEMI-CIRCLE PIECES. CHOP THE FRESH CORIANDER. ADD THESE INGREDIENTS TO THE MIXING BOWL ALONG WITH THE BABY SPINACH.
4. ADD THE SPROUTED PEAS AND BEANS TO THE MIXING BOWL WITH THE SESAME OIL, SESAME SEEDS, BALSAMIC VINEGAR AND SALT.
5. USE A SPOON (OR CLEAN HANDS) TO COMBINE THE INGREDIENTS TOGETHER.
6. SERVE AND GARNISH WITH SESAME SEEDS AND ENJOY!

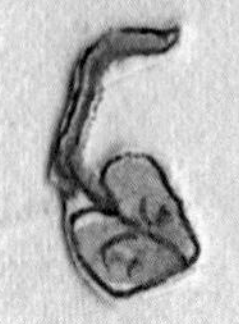

FYI!
RAW FOODS CAN CREATE GAS, BLOATING AND DISCOMFORT FOR VATA TYPES AND THOSE WITH WEAK AGNI (DIGESTIVE-FIRE), SO IT IS IMPORTANT FOR THEM TO GO EASY ON THE UNCOOKED GOODIES...
ALTOUGH, WE SHOULD ALL BE AWARE OF WHAT TYPE OF FOOD AND DRINK SUITS THE SEASON AND WEATHER EACH AND EVERY DAY!
SPROUTING NOTE
THESE SPROUTS ONLY NEED A DAY OR TWO OF SPROUTING (UNTIL THEY SWELL / BECOME-ACTIVATED)

10 MINUTES

LATE WINTER, SPRING

K-VP+

SERVES 2

balsamic KALETTES

INGREDIENTS

7 ASPARAGUS SPEARS
10 KALETTES OR...
300g CURLY KALE
1 TBSP COCONUT OIL
2 TBSP ORGANIC BALSAMIC VINEGAR
3 PINCHES HIMALAYAN SALT
3 PINCHES BLACK PEPPER

METHOD

1. CHOP THE ASPARAGUS INTO THIRDS OR THE CURLY KALE INTO 4CM CHUNKS.

2. HEAT THE COCONUT OIL IN A CAST IRON SKILLET ON A LOW-MEDIUM HEAT.

3. ADD THE ASPARAGUS, KALETTES OR KALE, BALSAMIC VINEGAR, SALT AND BLACK PEPPER TO THE SKILLET AND GIVE IT A STIR! COVER WITH A LID AND COOK FOR 4 MINUTES.

4. SERVE AS A SIDE TO A BIG BITE!

FYI!
KALE HAS BITTER AND ASTRINGENT QUALITIES THAT HELP TO DETOXIFY THE BODY, PARTICULARLY IN SPRING TIME. (KAPHA SEASON)

THE ORIGINAL STIR-FRY

30MINUTES SERVES 2 AUTUMN, WINTER, SPRING

INGREDIENTS

75g MATURE COCONUT FLESH
3 THUMBS GINGER ROOT
2 RED HOT CHILLIS
1 MEDIUM BROCCOLIS
1 LONG RED PEPPER
100g MANGETOUT
3 SPRING ONIONS
0.5 HANDFUL FRESH CORIANDER

2 TBSP COCONUT OIL
1 TSP CUMIN SEEDS
250mL ORGANIC COCONUT MILK
1.5 TSP BLACK PEPPER
3 TBSP ORGANIC TAMARI SAUCE

METHOD

1. SLICE THE COCONUT FLESH AND PEELED GINGER INTO THIN STRIPS. HEAT THE COCONUT OIL IN A WOK ON MEDIUM HEAT AND ADD THE COCONUT AND GINGER, ALONG WITH THE CUMIN SEEDS. STIR-FRY FOR 2 MINUTES.
2. DICE THE CHILLIS AND ADD THESE TO THE WOK WITH THE COCONUT MILK. STIR-FRY FOR ANOTHER 2 MINUTES.
3. CHOP THE BROCCOLI INTO SMALL FLORETS AND CUT THE LONG RED PEPPERS INTO 1 CM SECTIONS. ADD THESE TO THE WOK ALONG WITH THE MANGETOUT, TAMARI SAUCE AND BLACK PEPPER. STIR FOR 1 MINUTE.
4. COVER WITH THE WOK LID FOR 2 MINUTES, STIR AGAIN TO PREVENT STICKING OR BURNING. COVER FOR A FURTHER 3 MINUTES. TURN OFF THE HEAT AND KEEP IT COVERED.
5. CHOP THE CORIANDER AND SPRING ONION FINELY AND STIR THEM INTO THE WOK MIX. COVER AND LET IT STAND FOR 3-4 MINUTES.
6. SERVE WITH THE 'PERFECTLY FLUFFY RICE' RECIPE FOR A FULL, BALANCED MEAL!

S GF V

NO-FAFF FALAFFIES

AND TAHINI DRESSING

VPK~

ALL YEAR ROUND

1 HOUR, 30 MINUTES

MAKES 12 - 14 FALAFFIES

INGREDIENTS

130g MATURE COCONUT FLESH
300g SPROUTED MUNG BEANS
25g FRESH PARSLEY
20g FRESH MINT
20g FRESH CORIANDER
1 RED BELL PEPPER
2 RED HOT CHILLIS
0.5 LEMON (JUICE)

3 TBSP OLIVE OIL
100g GROUND ALMONDS (DRY)

1.5 TSP CORIANDER SEEDS
1.5 TSP CUMIN SEEDS
1.5 TSP SPIRULINA
1 TSP GROUND GINGER POWDER
1 TSP HIMALAYAN SALT
1 TSP BLACK PEPPER
0.25 TSP CAYENNE PEPPER

METHOD

* SPROUT THE MUNG BEANS USING THE 'SPROUTING (ALMOST) ANYTHING' RECIPE BEFORE BEGINNING THIS RECIPE. IF YOU DONT HAVE TIME TO SPROUT, YOU CAN SOAK THE MUNG INSTEAD FOR 1 HOUR AND THEN BOIL THEM FOR 30 MINUTES, OR UNTIL THEY ARE SOFT.

①

PRE-HEAT THE OVEN TO 180°C.

②

CRACK THE COCONUT AND CAREFULLY REMOVE THE FLESH FROM THE SHELL. CHOP THE FLESH INTO 1CM PIECES. CHOP THE BELL PEPPER SIMILARLY. FINELY CHOP THE PARSLEY, MINT, CORIANDER AND CHILLIS.

③

ADD THESE INGREDIENTS, ALONG WITH THE MUNG BEANS, LEMON JUICE, OLIVE OIL, CORIANDER AND CUMIN SEEDS INTO A BLENDER OR FOOD PROCESSOR. IF YOU ARE USING A BLENDER, YOU MAY WISH TO BLEND THE MIX IN 2 BATCHES. PULSE TO BLEND FOR 1-2 MINUTES OR UNTIL WELL PROCESSED, LEAVING SOME LUMPS FOR TEXTURE.

④

ADD THE BLENDED MIXTURE INTO A MIXING BOWL AND SPRINKLE OVER THE SPIRULINA, GINGER, SALT, PEPPER, CAYENNE AND 50g OF GROUND ALMONDS. USE YOUR CLEAN HANDS TO MASSAGE THE MIXTURE TOGETHER UNTIL IT IS THOROUGHLY COMBINED.

⑤

PREPARE A BAKING TRAY LINED WITH BAKING PAPER. SET ASIDE A SMALL BOWL OF THE REMAINING GROUND ALMONDS. CAREFULLY FASHION THE MIXTURE INTO 3-4CM WIDE BALLS AND ROLL THEM INTO THE ALMONDS TO COAT THEM, BEFORE POPPING THEM ON TO THE BAKING TRAY. PUSH THEM DOWN SO THAT THEY FLATTEN SLIGHTLY, WHICH HELPS THEM COOK MORE THOROUGHLY.

⑥

POP THEM IN THE OVEN FOR 25-30 MINUTES, CHECKING TO MAKE SURE THEY DO NOT BURN. THEY SHOULD BE NICELY GOLDEN AND BROWNING.

IF YOU PREFER THEM MORE SOLID, KEEP THEM IN THE OVEN FOR A LITTLE WHILE LONGER. CHECK THEM FREQUENTLY!

DIP INTO THE TAHINI DRESSING FOR EXTRA YUMMS.

THESE HEALTHY NO-FRY FALAFELS WILL HAVE YOU WANTING TO EAT THEM ALL DAY, EVERY DAY...
BUT! REMEMBER: "EVERYTHING IN MODERATION" LEADS TO A LIFE OF BALANCE.
FYI!
USING MUNG BEANS COMBINED WITH THE SPICES MAKES THE FALAFELS MUCH EASIER TO DIGEST THAN YOUR REGULAR FALAFELS.

VP-K+ ALL YEAR ROUND 10 MINUTES MAKES 400ML

TAHINI

DRESSING

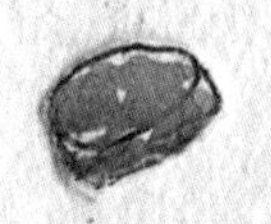

INGREDIENTS

15g	FRESH PARSLEY
0.5	LEMON (JUICE)
6 TBSP	ORGANIC TAHINI
1 TBSP	OLIVE OIL
0.25 TSP	HIMALAYAN SALT
200ML	FILTERED WATER

METHOD

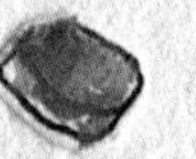

1. CHOP THE PARSLEY AND ADD IT TO THE BLENDER OR FOOD PROCESSOR WITH THE LEMON JUICE, TAHINI, OLIVE OIL, SALT AND WATER.

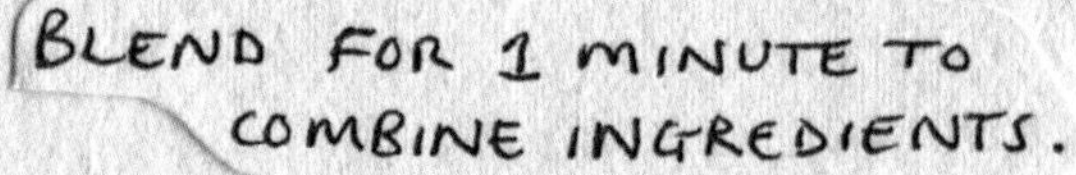

BLEND FOR 1 MINUTE TO COMBINE INGREDIENTS.

2. POUR INTO A JAR AND KEEP FOR UP TO 3 DAYS — YUM!

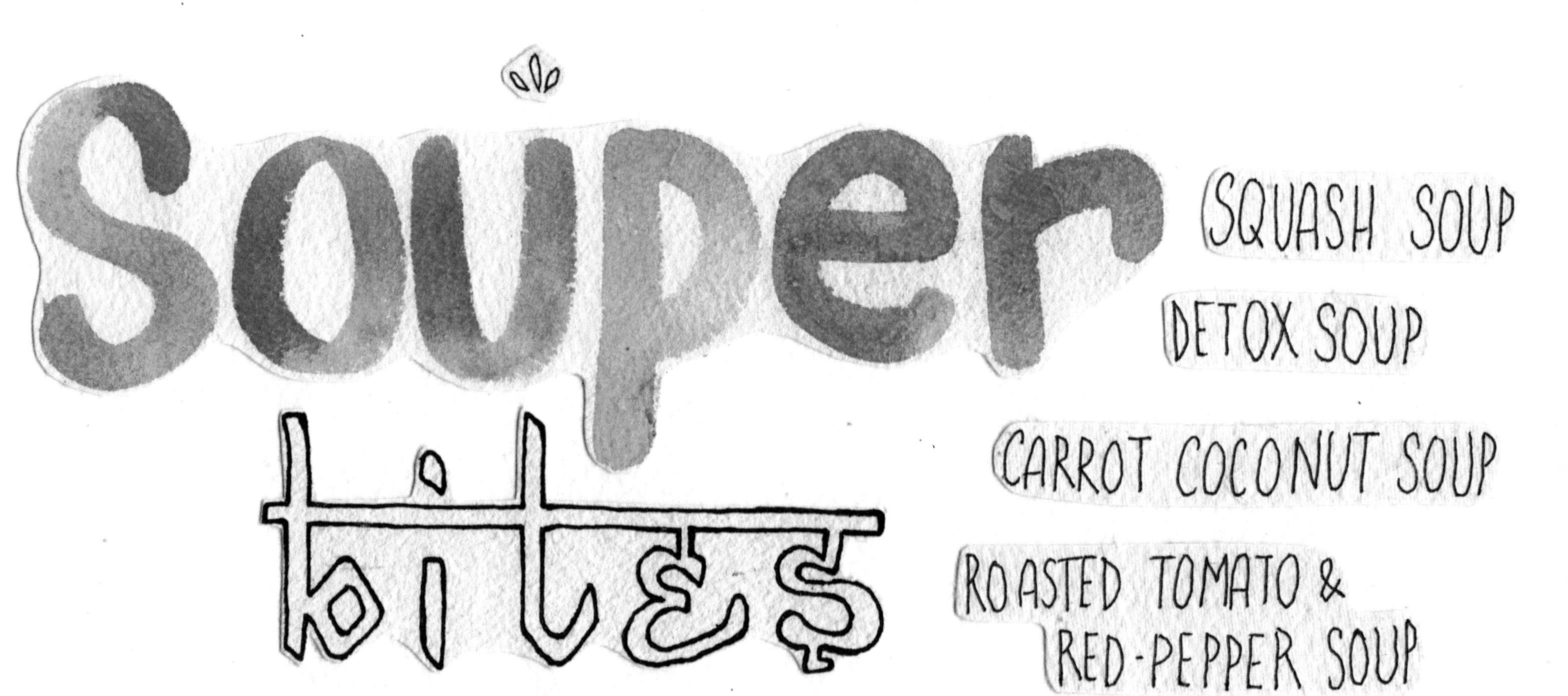

MISO-MISO BROTH

LEEK & POTATO SOUP

BROCCOLI & CARROT SOUP

ROOTSY GINGER SOUP

Ingredients

750g	SMALL	NEW POTATOES
1	SMALL	ONION
1	LARGE	SQUASH
3	LONG	RED PEPPERS
4	STICKS	CELERY
4	SPRIGS	FRESH ROSEMARY

2TBSP	OLIVE OIL
500ML	FILTERED WATER
0·5 TSP	CUMIN SEEDS
1 TSP	CARAWAY SEEDS
6 PODS	CARDAMOM
1 TSP	HIMALAYAN SALT
1 TSP	BLACK PEPPER.

SUMMER, AUTUMN EARLY WINTER

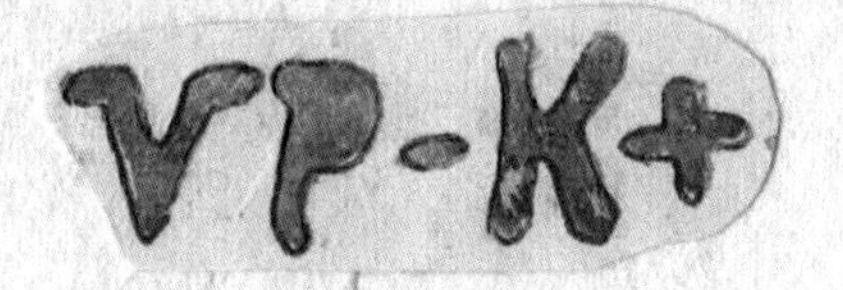

SERVES 4

1 HOUR

METHOD

1. HALVE THE POTATOES AND CHOP THE CELERY, PEPPERS AND ONION INTO 1CM PIECES. PEEL AND CHOP THE SQUASH INTO 2CM CUBES.

2. HEAT UP THE OLIVE OIL ON LOW IN A LARGE POT. ADD THESE INGREDIENTS TO THE POT AND COVER TO LET THE VEG SWEAT FOR 10 MINUTES, STIRRING OCCASIONALLY.

3. USING A PESTLE AND MORTAR, GRIND THE CUMIN AND CARAWAY SEEDS. BASH THE CARDAMOM PODS TO RELEASE THE SEEDS. DISCARD THE GREEN OUTER CASING.

4. ADD THE SPICES TO THE POT ALONG WITH THE SALT AND PEPPER AND CHOPPED ROSEMARY. STIR INTO THE MIXTURE AND COVER TO SWEAT FOR ANOTHER 5 MINUTES.

5. BOIL THE WATER AND ADD ENOUGH OF THIS TO THE POT TO COVER THE VEG. BRING THE MIXTURE TO BOIL ON A MEDIUM-LOW HEAT AND THEN REDUCE THE HEAT TO SIMMER FOR 15-20 MINUTES OR UNTIL THE POTATOES ARE SOFT. TURN OFF THE HEAT.

6. USING A HAND BLENDER, PAR-BLEND THE MIXTURE TO YOUR DESIRED CONSISTENCY. LEAVE FOR 5 MINUTES TO SLIGHTLY COOL BEFORE SERVING.

SO SIMPLE AND EASY TO DIGEST, THIS SOUP IS OUR ALLTIME FAVOURITE!
THE GINGER AND CARDAMOM ARE BRILLIANT FOR AIDING DIGESTION, AND INCREASING AGNI (THE DIGESTIVE FIRE).
FYI!

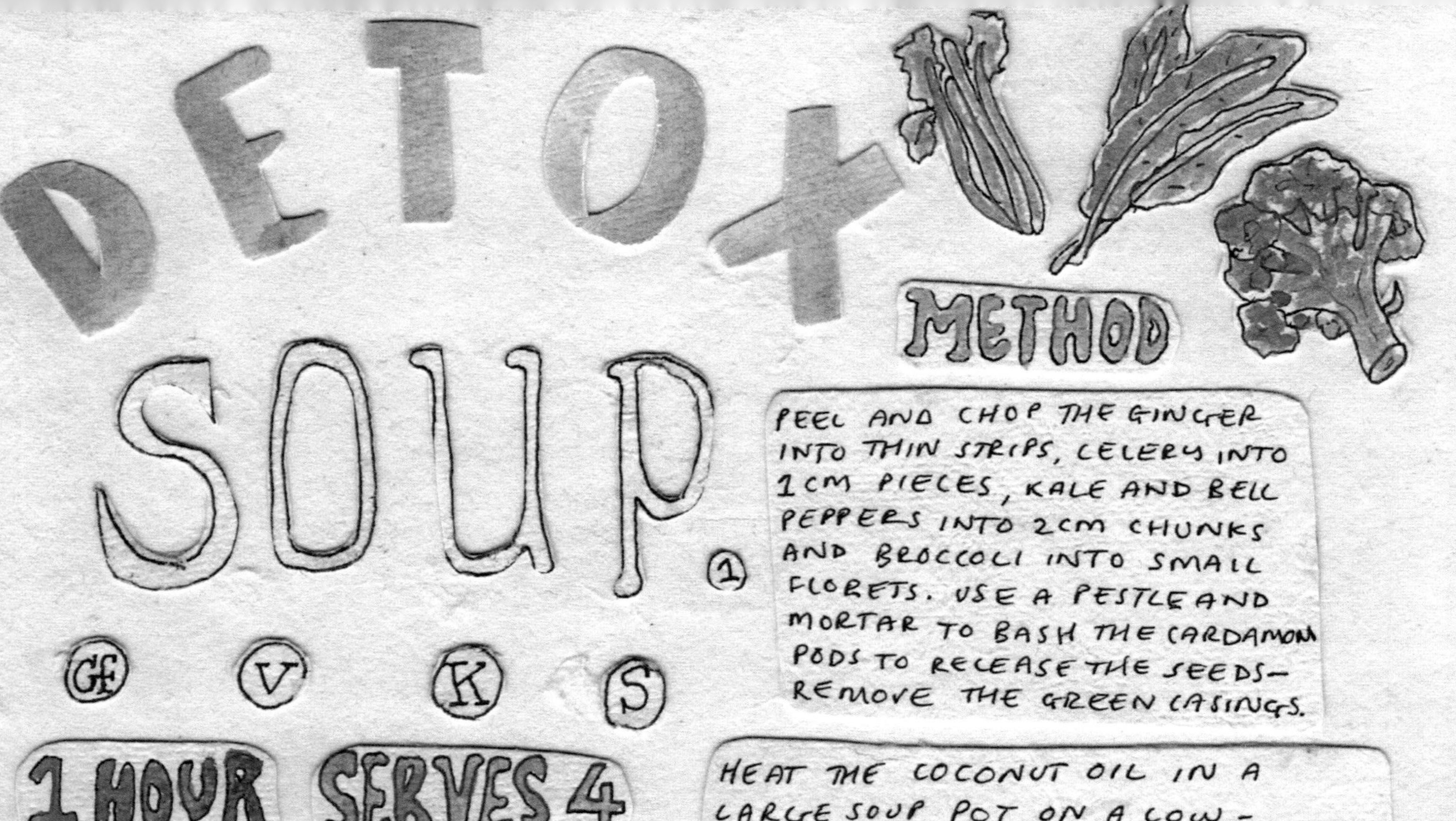

DETOX SOUP

GF V K S

1 HOUR SERVES 4

VPK↓

ALL YEAR ROUND

INGREDIENTS

- 2 THUMBS GINGER
- 10 STICKS CELERY
- 200g KALE
- 1 RED BELL PEPPER
- 1 GREEN BELL PEPPER
- 1.5 MEDIUM BROCCOLI
- 20g FRESH BASIL
- 1 HANDFUL FRESH CORIANDER
- 2 TBSP COCONUT OIL
- 7 PODS CARDAMOM
- 1 TSP CUMIN SEEDS
- 1 TSP HIMALAYAN SALT
- 1 TSP BLACK PEPPER
- 1L FILTERED WATER

+ OPTIONAL 150g MUNG BEAN (SPROUTED)

METHOD

1. PEEL AND CHOP THE GINGER INTO THIN STRIPS, CELERY INTO 1CM PIECES, KALE AND BELL PEPPERS INTO 2CM CHUNKS AND BROCCOLI INTO SMALL FLORETS. USE A PESTLE AND MORTAR TO BASH THE CARDAMOM PODS TO RELEASE THE SEEDS – REMOVE THE GREEN CASINGS.
2. HEAT THE COCONUT OIL IN A LARGE SOUP POT ON A LOW-HEAT. ADD THE CARDOMOM AND CUMIN SEEDS, SALT AND PEPPER. BETWEEN STIRS, ADD THE VEGGIES INTERMITTENTLY AND COAT THE VEG WITH THE OIL AND SPICES. PLACE THE LID ON AND SWEAT THE VEG FOR 15 MINUTES, STIRRING OCCASIONALLY TO PREVENT STICKING.
3. BOIL THE FILTERED WATER AND ADD ENOUGH TO THE POT TO ALMOST COVER THE VEG. TURN THE HEAT TO MEDIUM, BRING TO BOIL, THEN TURN THE HEAT BACK TO LOW TO SIMMER FOR ANOTHER 15 MINUTES.
4. TURN OFF THE HEAT. CHOP THE FRESH BASIL AND CORIANDER AND STIR THEM IN TO THE MIX. USE A HAND-BLENDER TO PAR-BLEND THE SOUP TO YOUR DESIRED CONSISTENCY.
5. LEAVE TO STAND WITH THE LID ON FOR 20 MINUTES BEFORE SERVING. GARNISH WITH FRESH CORIANDER AND SPROUTED MUNG BEANS.

ENJOY!

coriander
A GREAT HERB TO SOOTHE THE DIGESTION OF THE FOOD IT IS SERVED WITH!
carrots
CARROTS ARE EASY TO DIGEST AND GREAT FOR BOOSTING YOUR ENERGY. THEY PURIFY THE BLOOD AND ARE STRONGLY ALKALISING. THEY ALSO STABILISE SUGAR LEVELS BUT ARE BEST AVOIDED BY THOSE WITH CANDIDA OR OTHER SUGAR SENSITIVITIES.

Ingredients

5 LARGE CARROTS
2 MEDIUM PARSNIPS
6 STICKS CELERY
1 HANDFUL FRESH CORIANDER

2 TBSP COCONUT OIL
400ML ORGANIC COCONUT MILK
200-300ML FILTERED WATER
0.75 TSP HIMALAYAN SALT
0.5 TSP BLACK PEPPER
1 TSP CORIANDER SEEDS

Method

1. CHOP THE CARROTS, PARSNIP, AND CELERY. HEAT THE COCONUT OIL ON A LOW HEAT IN A POT AND ADD THE CHOPPED VEGGIES WITH THE SALT AND PEPPER. STIR TO COAT THE VEGGIES. POP THE LID ON THE POT AND SWEAT THE MIXTURE FOR 10 MINUTES, STIRRING OCCASIONALLY.

2. ADD THE COCONUT MILK AND ENOUGH WATER TO COVER THE VEGGIES. TURN THE HEAT TO MEDIUM FOR 5 MINUTES, THEN REDUCE THE HEAT TO SIMMER FOR 20 MINUTES, OR UNTIL THE VEGGIES ARE SOFT. THEN TURN OFF THE HEAT.

3. CHOP THE FRESH CORIANDER AND USE A PESTLE AND MORTAR TO GRIND THE CORIANDER SEEDS. ADD BOTH TO THE POT AND STIR THEM IN.

4. USING A HAND BLENDER, BLEND AROUND HALF OF THE SOUP, KEEPING SOME YUMMY CHUNKS!

5. SERVE AND GARNISH WITH FRESH CORIANDER.

ROASTED TOMATO & RED-PEPPER SOUP

GF 

VP+K-

1 HOUR

SERVES 4

LATE WINTER, SPRING

INGREDIENTS

8 LARGE	VINE TOMATOES
2 LARGE	RED BELL PEPPERS
70g	GRATED GINGER
300g	CURLEY KALE
20g	FRESH BASIL
30g	FRESH PARSLEY

5 TBSP	OLIVE OIL
700ML	FILTERED WATER
2 TSP	SMOKED PAPRIKA
1 TSP	HIMALAYAN SALT
1 TSP	BLACK PEPPER.

METHOD

① PRE-HEAT THE OVEN TO 180°C

CUT THE TOMATOES IN HALF AND THE PEPPERS INTO CHUNKS. PLACE THESE SKIN-DOWN ON BAKING PAPER LINED BAKING TRAYS. DRIZZLE WITH OLIVE OIL AND ROAST IN THE OVEN FOR 20-22 MINUTES, UNTIL THEY BEGIN TO BROWN SLIGHTLY.

② WHEN THERE IS JUST 5 MINUTES LEFT FOR THE VEG IN THE OVEN, HEAT THE REMAINING OLIVE OIL IN A LARGE POT ON A LOW HEAT FOR 5 MINUTES. ADD THE GRATED GINGER AND STIR FREQUENTLY TO PREVENT STICKING.

③ ONCE COOKED, ADD THE TOMATOES AND PEPPERS, AND ANY JUICES ON THE BAKING TRAYS, TO THE POT WITH THE SMOKED PAPRIKA, SALT AND PEPPER. STIR AND COOK FOR 10 MINUTES.

④ CHOP THE KALE INTO 2cm PIECES AND BOIL THE WATER IN THE KETTLE. ADD THESE TO THE POT, MIX THEM IN TO SUBMERGE THE KALE, COOK FOR 10 MORE MINUTES. THEN TURN OFF THE HEAT.

⑤ CHOP THE FRESH BASIL AND PARSLEY, THEN MIX THEM INTO THE POT. COVER WITH THE POT'S LID AND LET THE SOUP STAND FOR 15 MINUTES.

⑥ BLEND AROUND A THIRD OF THE INGREDIENTS USING A HAND BLENDER. TO SERVE, GARNISH WITH FRESH PARSLEY AND ENJOY!

FYI!
ADDING FRESH HERBS AT THE END OF COOKING AND LETTING THEM STAND WITH THE HEAT TURNED OFF WILL HELP TO PRESERVE THEIR FLAVOUR.
TOMATOES AND OTHER NIGHT-SHADES SUCH AS POTATOES, AUBERGINES AND ONIONS CAN BE OVERSTIMULATING.
IN EXCESS, THESE TYPES OF FOOD CAN EVEN LEAD TO STRESS AND ANXIETY... BUT WE LOVE THEM IN MODERATION! :)

FYI!
MISO HELPS TO HEAT UP OUR 'AGNI' (DIGESTIVE FIRE), SO IT IS GREAT FOR THOSE COLDER SEASONS.
AS IT IS FERMENTED, MISO IS WONDERFUL FOR OUR GUT HEALTH, WITH ALL THOSE NATURAL PROBIOTICS!
IF YOU'RE TIGHT ON TIME OUR 'MISO MISO' IS FOR YOU!
TAHINI IS GREAT FOR VATA BODY TYPES AND SEASONS AS IT IS HEAVY IN NATURE – MEANING IT IS TONIFYING; HELPING TO BUILD THE BODY UP, ESPECIALLY THE NERVOUS, MUSCLE AND FAT TISSUES.

AUTUMN and EARLY WINTER SERVES 2 40 MINS

V- PK+

INGREDIENTS

2 THUMBS	GINGER (GRATED)
2	SPRING ONIONS
2 SMALL	RED CHILLIS
300g	TENDER STEM BROCCOLI
0.5	CONEHEAD CABBAGE
1 TBSP	ORGANIC TAHINI
2 TBSP	COCONUT OIL
1.5L	FILTERED WATER.
1 TBSP	ORGANIC AGED MISO PASTE
2 TBSP	MUSTARD SEEDS
0.5TSP	HIMALAYAN SALT
1 TSP	BLACK PEPPER.

METHOD

GRATE THE GINGER AND HEAT THE OIL IN A MEDIUM SIZED POT ON A LOW-MEDIUM HEAT.

ADD THE GINGER TO COOK FOR 6 MINUTES. STIR TO PREVENT STICKING.

①

ROUGHLY CHOP THE SPRING ONION AND CHILLIS TO ADD THEM WITH THE MUSTARD SEEDS, SALT, PEPPER AND WATER TO THE POT.

COOK ON A MEDIUM HEAT FOR ANOTHER 8 MINUTES TO MAKE A BROTH.

②

③

CHOP THE CABBAGE ROUGHLY INTO 1CM-WIDE STRIPS. ADD THESE, ALONG WITH THE BROCCOLI STEMS TO THE BROTH.

COOK FOR 4 MINUTES THEN TURN OFF THE HEAT TO LET THE BROTH STAND FOR 10 MINUTES.

ONCE THE BROTH HAS SLIGHTLY COOLED, ADD THE MISO AND TAHINI TO SERVE. STIR THE BROTH TO ALLOW THESE INGREDIENTS TO DISSOLVE.

SERVE AND ENJOY!

LEEK & POTATO SOUP

METHOD

1. CHOP THE POTATOES INTO 2CM CUBES AND SLICE THE LEEKS INTO 2CM CHUNKS. HEAT THE OIL IN A LARGE POT ON A LOW HEAT AND ADD THE POTATOES, LEEKS, SALT, CUMIN SEEDS, PEPPER AND ASWAGANDA. COVER AND SWEAT THE VEGGIES FOR 15 MINUTES, STIRRING OCCASIONALLY TO PREVENT STICKING.

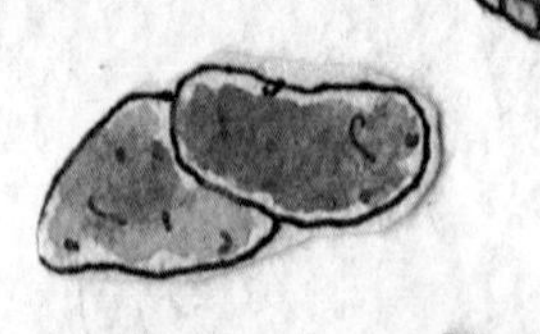

INGREDIENTS

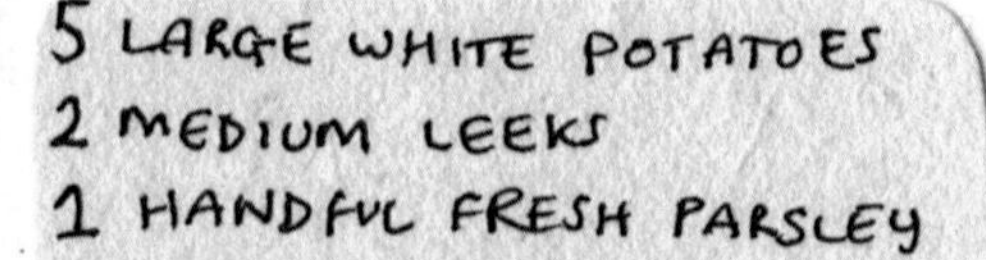

5 LARGE WHITE POTATOES
2 MEDIUM LEEKS
1 HANDFUL FRESH PARSLEY

2 TBSP COCONUT OIL
1 TSP HIMALAYAN SALT
1 TSP CUMIN SEEDS
1 TSP BLACK PEPPER
1 TSP ASWAGANDA
6-800ML FILTERED WATER
1 TSP CORIANDER SEEDS

45 MINUTES

2. BOIL THE WATER AND ADD TO THE POT (ENOUGH TO ALMOST COVER THE VEG.) STIR AND BRING TO BOIL ON A MEDIUM HEAT, LEAVING TO SIMMER WITH THE LID ON FOR A FURTHER 20 MINUTES OR UNTIL THE VEGGIES ARE SOFT.

SERVES 4

3. TURN OFF THE HEAT. CHOP THE PARSLEY AND GRIND THE CORIANDER SEEDS USING A PASTEL AND MORTAR. ADD THESE TO THE POT. WITH A HAND BLENDER, PAR-BLEND THE SOUP UNTIL IT IS A DESIRED THICKNESS - (WE USUALLY BLEND AROUND HALF OF THE VEG FOR A NICE CHUNKY TEXTURE).

ALL YEAR ROUND

4. GARNISH WITH MORE PARSLEY AND ENJOY!

MAMA'S SOUP
A FAMILY CLASSIC THAT OUR MOTHER HAS MADE SINCE BEFORE WE COULD REMEMBER...
IT'S A WHOLESOME, GROUNDING AND HOMELY DISH WHEN YOU NEED A BIT OF WARMTH AND COMFORT IN YOUR LIFE!

FYI!

DON'T WASTE THE BROCCOLI STEM - ITS THE TASTIEST AND MOST NUTRITIOUS PART!

THE STEM IS WHERE ALL THE 'GOOD STUFF' TRAVELS TO THE FLORETS.

WE CAN'T DISCOUNT THEIR GOODNESS, EVEN IF THEY COME WITH MORE OF A CRUNCH!!

GF V

VPK+

45 MINUTES SERVES 2 ALL YEAR ROUND

broccoli and carrot SOUP

INGREDIENTS

4 LARGE	CARROTS
1 MEDIUM	LEEK
3 STICKS	CELERY
1 MEDIUM	BROCCOLI
2 THUMBS	GINGER
25g	FRESH CORIANDER

2 TBSP	COCONUT OIL
1.5 TSP	CARAWAY SEEDS
0.5 TSP	BLACK PEPPER
0.5 TSP	HIMALAYAN SALT
500-600ML	FILTERED WATER

METHOD

1. CHOP THE CARROTS, LEEK AND CELERY INTO 1.5CM CHUNKS, PEEL AND GRATE THE GINGER AND CHOP THE BROCCOLI AND STEM INTO SMALL FLORETS OR STRIPS.

2. HEAT THE OIL IN A POT ON A LOW HEAT AND ADD THE ABOVE INGREDIENTS ALONG WITH THE CARAWAY SEEDS, PEPPER AND SALT. PUT THE LID ON AND SWEAT THE VEGGIES FOR 15 MINUTES, STIRRING OCCASIONALLY.

3. BOIL THE WATER AND ADD ENOUGH TO ALMOST COVER THE VEGGIES IN THE POT. BRING TO BOIL ON A MEDIUM HEAT THEN TURN DOWN TO SIMMER FOR 15-20 MORE MINUTES, OR UNTIL THE VEGGIES ARE COOKED TO YOUR LIKING.

4. TURN OFF THE HEAT, CHOP AND ADD THE FRESH CORIANDER TO THE POT AND USE A HAND BLENDER TO PAR-BLEND THE SOUP.

5. LEAVE TO COOL FOR 5 MINUTES BEFORE DISHING UP AND GARNISHING WITH FRESH CORIANDER!

THIS IS AN AWESOME ONE-POTTER THAT IS 'SOUPER' GROUNDING.

WE LEARNT THIS METHOD OF SOUP COOKING FROM OUR MUM...

CHOP → SWEAT → BOIL → BLEND → ENJOY!

ASHWAGANDHA

ASHWAGANDHA IS A MIRICLE HERB. IT IS AN ADAPTOGEN SO IT HELPS TO REDUCE STRESS AND LEADS TO IMPROVED BLOOD SUGAR LEVELS, REDUCED INFLAMMATION, IMPROVED MOOD, MEMORY AND OVERALL WELL-BEING!

ROOTSY GINGER

GF V

45 MINUTES

SERVES 4

ALL YEAR ROUND

VPKu

INGREDIENTS

- 3 TBSP COCONUT OIL
- 3 MEDIUM SWEET POTATOES
- 4 MEDIUM CARROTS
- 2 MEDIUM LEEKS
- 3 THUMBS GINGER ROOT
- 1 THUMB TUMERIC ROOT
  OR 1.5 TSP TUMERIC POWDER
- 6-800ML FILTERED WATER

- 1 TSP HIMALAYAN SALT
- 1.5 TSP BLACK PEPPER
- 1.5 TSP CUMIN SEEDS
- 1 TSP CORIANDER SEEDS (GROUND)
- 2 TSP ASHWAGANDHA POWDER

METHOD

1. CHOP THE SWEET POTATOES INTO 2CM CUBES, CARROTS AND LEEKS INTO 1CM SLICES, AND GRATE THE GINGER AND TUMERIC. HEAT THE COCONUT OIL ON A LOW HEAT IN A LARGE POT. ADD ALL THESE INGREDIENTS TO THE POT, STIRRING THEM INTO THE OIL. MAKE SURE THAT THE GINGER AND TUMERIC DO NOT STICK TO THE BASE OF THE POT. SWEAT THE VEG FOR 15 MINUTES, STIRRING OCCASIONALLY.
2. ADD THE SALT, PEPPER, CUMIN, CORIANDER AND ASHWAGANDHA AND STIR THEM INTO THE MIXTURE FOR AROUND 2 MINUTES.
3. BOIL THE WATER AND ADD ENOUGH OF IT TO ALMOST COVER THE VEG IN THE POT. BRING TO SIMMER OVER A LOW - MEDIUM HEAT FOR ANOTHER 20 MINUTES, UNTIL THE VEG IS SOFT.
4. ONCE COOKED, REMOVE THE POT FROM THE HEAT AND, USING A HAND BLENDER, BLEND HALF OF THE SOUP TO CREATE A THICK CONSISTENCY.
5. GARNISH WITH FRESH CORIANDER AND ENJOY!

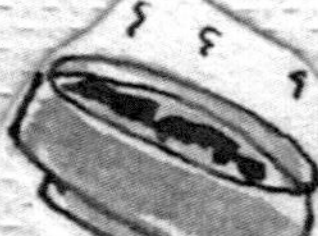

big bites
BANGIN' DRY DAL
POPEYE PIE
'LANKI CURRY
PEARL BEET POT
SUPA GREEN CURRY
BANGIN' WET DAL
SATISFRYING RICE
KITCHARI
SPROUTED PLANT CHILLI
RATA-TOUI
THE SWEETEST POTATO PIE
CURRY NO.3
BIG PASTIES
POHA

bangin' dry dal
GF
V
INGREDIENTS
400g CHERRY TOMATOES
2 LONG RED PEPPERS
0.75 LEMON (JUICE)
0.5 HANDFUL FRESH CORIANDER
4 TBSP GRATED COCONUTFLESH
4 RED HOT CHILLIS
2 THUMBS FRESH GINGER ROOT
2 THUMBS FRESH TUMERIC ROOT
2 TBSP COCONUT OIL
900 ML FILTERED WATER
400g DARK SPECKLED LENTILS (DRY)
1 CAN ORGANIC COCONUT MILK
6 BAY LEAVES
2 TSP MUSTARD SEEDS
1.5 TSP CUMIN SEEDS
1.5 TSP GARAM MASALA
8 CURRY LEAVES
1.5 TSP CORIANDER SEEDS.

SPRING & LATE WINTER

1 hour. 20 minutes

VP + K - SERVES 4

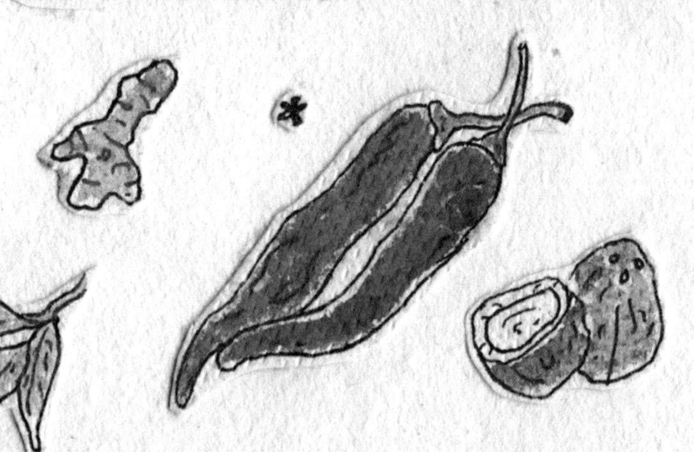

METHOD

1. HEAT THE COCONUT OIL IN A DEEP CAST-IRON PAN ON A MEDIUM HEAT. FRY THE MUSTARD AND CUMIN SEEDS FOR 2 MINUTES TO RELEASE THEIR AROMAS.

2. PEEL AND GRATE THE TUMERIC AND GINGER ROOT AND ADD THESE TO THE PAN. FRY FOR 3 MINUTES, MAKING SURE THEY DO NOT STICK TO THE PAN.

3. IN A BLENDER, BLEND THE CHERRY TOMATOES WITH THE FILTERED WATER FOR 1 MINUTE AND ADD THIS MIXTURE TO THE PAN.

4. ADD THE BAY LEAVES, CURRY LEAVES, CHOPPED CHILLIS, GARAM MASALA AND LENTILS TO THE PAN AND BRING TO SIMMER ON A MEDIUM HEAT. COOK FOR 30-45 MINUTES, STIRRING OCCASIONALLY. IF NEEDED, YOU MAY ADD EXTRA WATER TO THE MIXTURE IF THE LENTILS ARE DRY BUT ARE STILL UNCOOKED.

5. WHEN THE LENTILS ARE COOKED AND THE MIXTURE HAS BECOME DRY, CHOP THE RED-PEPPERS AND FRESH CORIANDER TO THEN ADD THESE TO THE PAN WITH THE COCONUT MILK, LEMON JUICE AND GROUND CORIANDER SEEDS. COOK ON A LOW HEAT FOR ANOTHER 5-10 MINUTES, STIRRING FREQUENTLY.

6. SERVE AND GARNISH WITH A SPRINKLE OF FRESH GRATED COCONUT!

popeye PIE

SERVES 6 2 HOURS

ALL YEAR VPK~

Ingredients

- 1.5 MEDIUM LEEKS
- 1 FENNEL BULB
- 10 SMALL NEW POTATOES
- 250g CURLY KALE (CAVOLO NERO)
- 500g BABY SPINACH
- 10 SPEARS ASPARAGUS
- 10g FRESH THYME
- 15g FRESH BASIL
- 2 TBSP OLIVE OIL
- 200 mL FILTERED WATER
- 1.5 TSP CUMIN SEEDS
- 1 TSP BLACK PEPPER
- 1 TSP HIMALAYAN SALT
- 1 'WHOLESOME WHOLEWHEAT PASTRY' RECIPE.

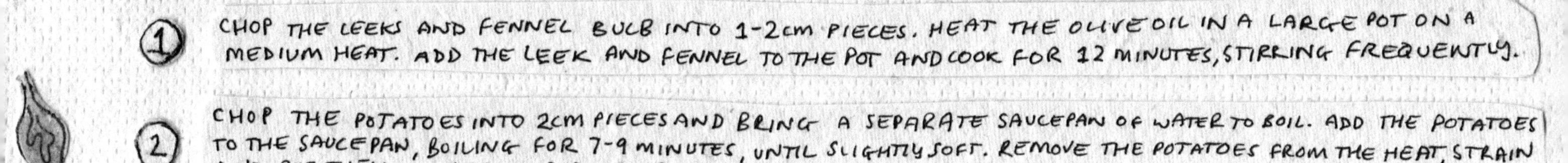

1. CHOP THE LEEKS AND FENNEL BULB INTO 1-2cm PIECES. HEAT THE OLIVE OIL IN A LARGE POT ON A MEDIUM HEAT. ADD THE LEEK AND FENNEL TO THE POT AND COOK FOR 12 MINUTES, STIRRING FREQUENTLY.

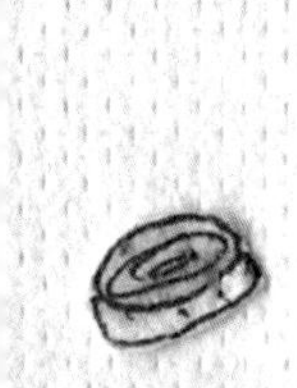

2. CHOP THE POTATOES INTO 2CM PIECES AND BRING A SEPARATE SAUCEPAN OF WATER TO BOIL. ADD THE POTATOES TO THE SAUCEPAN, BOILING FOR 7-9 MINUTES, UNTIL SLIGHTLY SOFT. REMOVE THE POTATOES FROM THE HEAT, STRAIN AND PUT THEM TO THE SIDE FOR LATER USE.

3. CHOP THE KALE AND ASPARAGUS INTO 2CM PIECES AND ADD THEM TO THE LEEK AND FENNEL POT, ALONG WITH THE SPINACH AND WATER. REDUCE THE HEAT TO LOW AND USE A WOODEN SPOON TO MIX IN THE LEAVES SO THAT THEY REDUCE IN VOLUME. YOU MAY WISH TO ADD THE SPINACH IN STAGES. COVER THE POT WITH A LID AND COOK FOR 10-15 MINUTES, STIRRING OCCASIONALLY.

4. TOAST THE CUMIN SEEDS LIGHTLY IN A SMALL FRYING PAN FOR 1 MINUTE TO RELEASE THE AROMAS, THEN REMOVE THEM FROM THE HEAT. CHOP THE FRESH THYME AND BASIL AND ADD THESE, WITH THE CUMIN SEEDS, BLACK PEPPER, SALT AND COOKED POTATOES TO THE LARGE POT. STIR WELL AND LEAVE TO COOK FOR ANOTHER 5 MINUTES.

5. REMOVE FROM THE HEAT AND ALLOW TO COOL, WHILST MAKING THE 'WHOLESOME WHOLEWHEAT PASTRY' RECIPE. PRE-HEAT THE OVEN TO 180°C.

6. USING A 26cm x 6cm PIE DISH, BEGIN BY GREASING THE SIDES WITH OLIVE OIL. THEN DIVIDE THE PASTRY DOUGH INTO TWO BALLS. USE A ROLLING PIN TO ROLL ONE BALL INTO A 36CM CIRCLE TO LINE THE BOTTOM OF THE DISH. GENTLY PRESS THE DOUGH INTO THE SIDES OF THE DISH AND TRIM OFF ANY OVER-HANG FROM THE DISH, LEAVING AROUND 1 CM OF PASTRY OVER THE EDGE OF THE DISH. WET THE UP-FACING LIP OF THE PASTRY, WHICH SITS ON THE EDGE OF THE DISH.

7. ADD THE VEG PIE MIXTURE TO THE LINED PIE DISH, USING A SLIT SPOON. TRY TO LEAVE AS MUCH JUICE FROM THE VEGGIES BEHIND TO REDUCE THE SOGGINESS OF THE PIE.

8. ROLL THE REMAINING BALL OF PASTRY INTO AN IDENTICAL 36cm CIRCLE AND GENTLY LAY IT OVER THE PIE TOP. USING YOUR FINGERS, PINCH THE WET EDGES AND 1CM OVER HANG OF THE BOTTOM PASTRY, SO THAT IT STICKS TO THE TOP PASTRY. YOU CAN TRIM THE EXCESS PASTRY TO FASHION SOME DELICATE DESIGNS TO PLACE ON THE TOP OF THE PIE. ATTACH THE DESIGNS WITH WATER. USE A FORK TO PIERCE HOLES INTO THE TOP PASTRY TO ALLOW ANY STEAM TO ESCAPE.

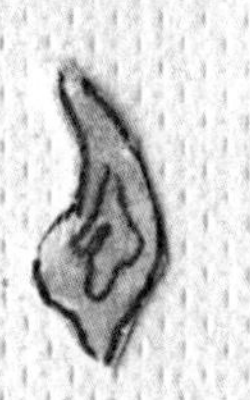

9. BRUSH THE PIE GENTLY WITH SOME ROOM TEMPERATURE WATER AND PLACE IT INTO THE OVEN FOR 30 MINUTES. IF YOU PREFER YOUR PIE SLIGHTLY MORE BROWNED YOU CAN LEAVE IT IN FOR A SHORT WHILE LONGER, CHECKING FREQUENTLY.

10. ALLOW THE PIE TO STAND FOR 5 MINUTES BEFORE SERVING AND ENJOYING YOUR CREATION!

IF YOU COULD CHANGE JUST ONE THING IN YOUR COOKING TO MAKE YOU AND YOUR FAMILY HEALTHIER, IT WOULD BE TO ENSURE YOUR CANNED FOODS, LIKE COCONUT MILK AND CHOPPED TOMATOES, ARE ORGANIC OR WITHOUT ADDITIVES.
A VERY BIG FYI!
ADDITIVES CAN MAKE A HEALTHY MEAL BAD FOR YOUR BODY SO WATCH OUT FOR THEM!
BE CREATIVE AND ADD YOUR OWN CHOICE OF VEGGIES!
IF YOU HAVE A GARDEN, BAY TREES ARE VERY EASY TO TAKE CARE OF AND ARE ABUNDANT IN PRODUCE!
YOU CAN'T BEAT TAKING CUTTINGS FROM YOUR OWN GARDEN AND THROWING THEM INTO YOUR MEAL FRESH!

'LANNKI CURRY

1 HOUR 15 MINUTES

SERVES 4

V

GF

FALL, WINTER, SPRING

VK-P+

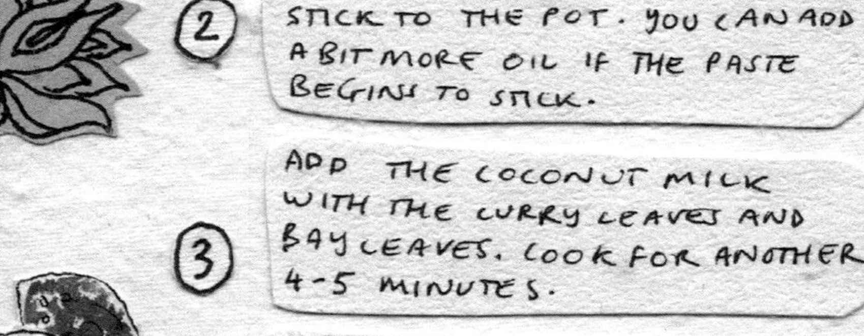

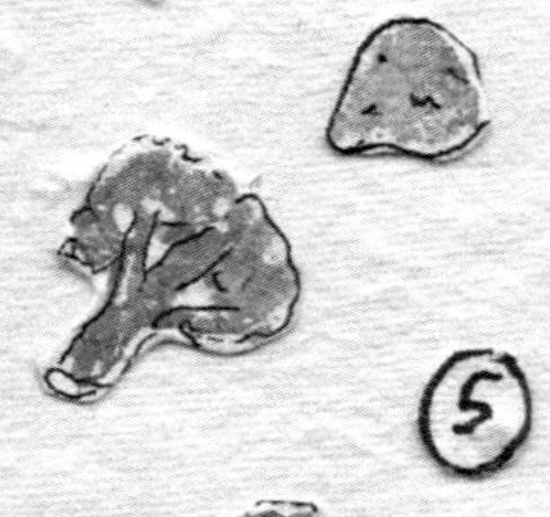

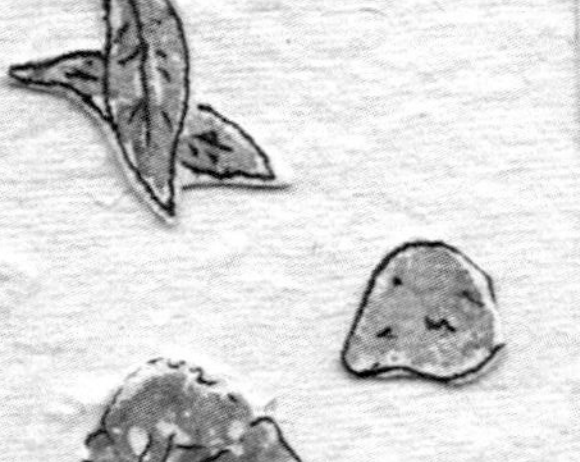

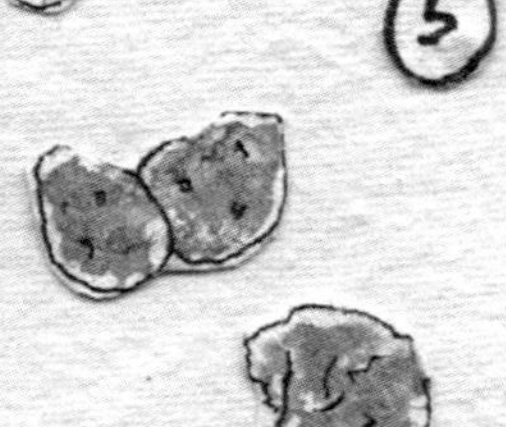

INGREDIENTS

1 MEDIUM	WHITE ONION
3 LARGE	PLUM TOMATOES
10 SMALL	NEW POTATOES
1 MEDIUM	BROCCOLI
2 TBSP	COCONUT OIL
250g	'SUPA GOLDEN PASTE'
0.5 CAN	ORGANIC COCONUT MILK
1 CAN	ORGANIC CHOPPED TOMATOES
300 ML	FILTERED WATER
1 TSP	MUSTARD SEEDS
6	BAY LEAVES
4	CURRY LEAVES
0.5 TSP	HIMALAYAN SALT
0.5 TSP	BLACK PEPPER

METHOD

1. CHOP THE ONIONS INTO THIN SLICES. HEAT THE OIL IN A LARGE POT ON A LOW-MEDIUM HEAT AND ADD THE ONIONS AND MUSTARD SEEDS, STIRRING FREQUENTLY FOR 10 MINUTES, UNTIL THE ONIONS ARE TRANSLUCENT.
2. ADD THE 'SUPA GOLDEN PASTE' AND STIR FOR 6 MINUTES, ENSURING THE MIX DOES NOT STICK TO THE POT. YOU CAN ADD A BIT MORE OIL IF THE PASTE BEGINS TO STICK.
3. ADD THE COCONUT MILK WITH THE CURRY LEAVES AND BAY LEAVES. COOK FOR ANOTHER 4-5 MINUTES.
4. CHOP THE PLUM TOMATOES INTO QUARTERS AND THE NEW POTATOES IN HALF. ADD THESE WITH THE CANNED TOMATOES AND WATER TO THE POT. BRING THE MIX TO BOIL, THEN REDUCE THE HEAT TO LOW, COVERING AND ALLOWING TO SIMMER FOR 15-20 MINUTES, OR UNTIL THE POTATOES ARE SOFT.
5. CHOP THE BROCCOLI HEAD INTO LARGE FLORETS, AND STEMS INTO STRIPS. ADD THESE, ALONG WITH THE SALT AND PEPPER TO THE POT, STIRRING TO SUBMERGE THE BROCCOLI INTO THE MIX. COVER AND SIMMER FOR 10 MINUTES.
6. TURN OFF THE HEAT AND LEAVE TO COOL FOR 30 MINUTES BEFORE GENTLY RE-HEATING TO SERVE (THIS ALLOWS THE FLAVOURS TO SOAK IN) — ENJOY!

BEETS

BEETS CONTAIN HIGH AMOUNTS OF FOLIC ACID AND HELP TO PROMOTE REGULAR MENSURATION IN WOMEN!

WITH A HEATING QUALITY, BEETS ARE NOURISHING AND ENERGISING - PROVING GREAT AS AN AID TO CONSTPATION AND TREATING HAEMORRHOIDS.

BARLEY

BARLEY IS ALSO A WINNER – A LAXATIVE, APHRODISIAC AND STAMINA STRENGTHENER...

(BUT HOPEFULLY NOT AT THE SAME TIME)

Pearl/Beet Pot

SERVES 4 | ALL YEAR

1 HOUR | VPKN

METHOD

1. CHOP THE CARROTS, SWEET POTATOES, BEETROOT, CELERY, KALE AND ZUCCHINI INTO EQUALLY SIZED CHUNKS. PEEL AND CHOP THE GINGER AND HERBS.

2. IN A LARGE POT, GENTLY FRY THE GROUND CORIANDER, CUMIN, MUSTARD SEEDS, CHILLI FLAKES AND BLACK PEPPER ON A LOW HEAT TO RELEASE THEIR AROMAS.

3. WHEN THE MUSTARD SEEDS BEGIN TO POP ADD THE OLIVE OIL, 250 ML OF WATER, CHOPPED HERBS AND VEGGIES, EXCEPT THE KALE, TO THE POT. COOK ON A LOW-MEDIUM HEAT FOR 5 MINUTES BEFORE ADDING THE CHOPPED TOMATOES. COOK FOR ANOTHER 10 MINUTES WITH THE LID ON, STIRRING OCCASIONALLY.

4. AFTER 10 MINUTES, ADD THE KALE AND, IF NEEDED, ENOUGH WATER TO JUST COVER THE VEGGIES. ADD THE PEARL BARLEY TO THE POT, STIRRING WELL TO SUBMERGE IT INTO THE VEG MIXTURE. REPLACE THE LID AND LEAVE TO SIMMER ON A MEDIUM HEAT FOR 30 MINUTES. REDUCE THE HEAT TO LOW IF THE POT IS BOILING. STIR OCCASIONALLY.

5. AFTER 30 MINUTES, TEST THE PEARL BARLEY TO SEE IF IT IS COOKED TO YOUR LIKING. IF SO, SERVE WITH A SPRINKLE OF FRESH CORIANDER!

INGREDIENTS

2 THUMBS GINGER
2 BEETROOTS
4 CARROTS
4 STALKS KALE
3 STALKS CELERY
1 ZUCCHINI
1 LARGE SWEET POTATOES

2 SPRIGS FRESH ROSEMARY
2 SPRIGS FRESH THYME
2 SPRIGS FRESH CORIANDER
2 SPRIGS FRESH OREGANO

250g PEARL BARLEY (DRY)
1 TSP OLIVE OIL
300ML FILTERED WATER
1 CAN ORGANIC CHOPPED TOMATOES

1 TSP GROUND CORIANDER
1 TSP GROUND CUMIN
1 TSP MUSTARD SEEDS
0.5 TSP CHILLI FLAKES
0.5 TSP BLACK PEPPER

SERVES 4 1·25 hours

VPK ~ ALL YEAR

INGREDIENTS

2 THUMBS	GINGER
1 STICK	LEMONGRASS
2 HOT	RED CHILLIS
400g	GREEN BEANS
2 LONG	RED BELL PEPPERS
1	BROCCOLI
10g	FRESH THAI BASIL
10g	FRESH CORIANDER

2TBSP	COCONUT OIL
250ML	'SUPA GREEN PASTE'
2CANS	ORGANIC COCONUT MILK
200ML	FILTERED WATER

1 TBSP	MUSTARD SEEDS
0·5 TSP	GROUND CINNAMON
5	KAFFIR LIME LEAVES
0·5 TSP	HIMALAYAN SALT
0·5 TSP	BLACK PEPPER
0·5 TSP	GROUND CORIANDER

METHOD

1. HEAT THE COCONUT OIL ON A LOW HEAT WITH THE MUSTARD SEEDS IN A POT FOR 2 MINUTES. THEN ADD THE 'SUPA GREEN PASTE' AND COOK WHILST STIRRING FOR 10 MINUTES UNTIL THE PASTE BECOMES A STICKY CONSISTENCY.

2. PEEL AND CHOP THE GINGER INTO CHUNKS AND REMOVE THE OUTER LEAVES OF THE LEMONGRASS. TURN THE HEAT TO LOW-MEDIUM AND ADD 1 CAN OF COCONUT MILK, ALONG WITH THE GINGER, LEMONGRASS, CHOPPED CHILLIS, CINNAMON, KAFFIR LIME LEAVES, SALT AND PEPPER TO THE POT. SIMMER FOR 4 MINUTES TO RELEASE THE FLAVOURS.

3. CHOP THE GREEN BEANS, RED PEPPERS AND BROCCOLI AND ADD THESE TO THE POT. ADD THE SECOND CAN OF COCONUT MILK AND THE WATER. STIR IN THE VEGGIES AND BRING THE MIXTURE TO BOIL.

4. TURN DOWN THE HEAT TO ALLOW THE POT TO SIMMER FOR 15-20 MINUTES, OR UNTIL THE VEG IS COOKED TO YOUR LIKING.

5. CHOP AND STIR IN THE FRESH BASIL, FRESH CORIANDER AND GROUND CORIANDER. TURN OFF THE HEAT AND LET THE CURRY STAND FOR 5 MINUTES.

6. GARNISH WITH A SPRINKLE OF FRESH CORIANDER AND SERVE ALONGSIDE OUR 'PERFECTLY FLUFFY RICE' RECIPE.

bangin' wet dal

3 TBSP	FRESH GINGER ROOT
3 TBSP	FRESH TUMERIC ROOT
5 LARGE	VINE TOMATOES
2 GREEN	HOT CHILLI PEPPERS
1 WHOLE	LIME (UNWAXED)
1 LONG	GREEN PEPPER
1 LONG	RED PEPPER
300g	BABY SPINACH
1 HANDFUL	FRESH CORIANDER
15g	FRESH BASIL
300g	MUNG BEANS (SOAKED) (OVERNIGHT)

2 TBSP	COCONUT OIL
1 CAN	ORGANIC COCONUT MILK
600ML	FILTERED WATER
0.5 TSP	HOT CHILLI POWDER
1.5 TSP	GARAM MASALA
1 TSP	PAPRIKA

METHOD

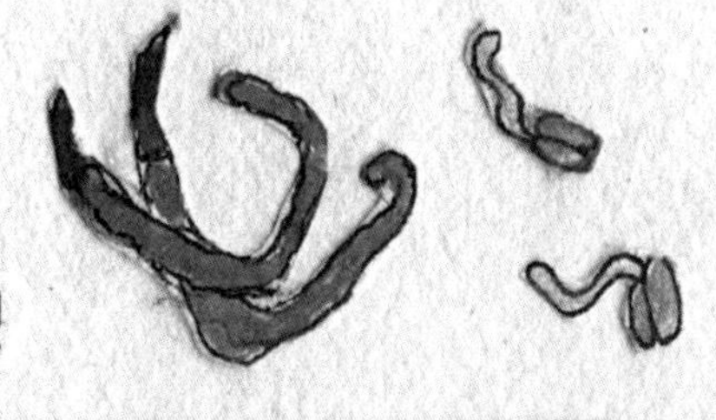

* SOAK THE MUNG OVERNIGHT!

SERVES 4

1 HOUR

ALL YEAR

VPK~

1. PEEL AND GRATE THE FRESH GINGER AND TUMERIC ROOT. HEAT THE OIL IN A LARGE POT ON A LOW HEAT AND ADD THE GRATED ROOTS WITH 50ML OF WATER. COOK FOR 8 MINUTES, STIRRING FREQUENTLY TO PREVENT STICKING.

2. ADD THE HOT CHILLI POWDER, GARAM MASALA, PAPRIKA AND ANOTHER 50ML OF WATER. STIR FOR ANOTHER 2 MINUTES.

3. CHOP THE TOMATOES INTO QUARTERS, THEN DICE THE HOT CHILLIS AND ADD THESE TO THE POT WITH THE SQUEEZED LIME. IF YOUR LIME IS CLEAN AND UNWAXED, ADD THE SQUEEZED SEGMENTS TO THE POT TOO. COOK FOR 8 MINUTES.

4. ADD THE SOAKED MUNG BEANS AND 500ML OF BOILED WATER TO THE POT. BRING TO BOIL AND THEN REDUCE TO SIMMER FOR ANOTHER 8 MINUTES.

5. SLICE THE GREEN AND RED PEPPERS AND ADD THESE WITH THE COCONUT MILK TO THE MIX, STIRRING AND LEAVING TO COOK FOR ANOTHER 8 MINUTES.

6. REMOVE THE POT FROM THE HEAT AND STIR IN THE SPINACH, CHOPPED FRESH CORIANDER AND FRESH BASIL USING A SPOON. LEAVE TO SIT FOR 15 MINUTES, STIRRING THE SPINACH ONCE OR TWICE TO MIX IT IN WELL.

7. GARNISH WITH A SPRINKLE OF FRESH CORIANDER AND SERVE BY ITSELF OR WITH ONE OF OUR RICE DISHES!

SATISFRYING
RICE

AUTUMN AND EARLY WINTER

1 HOUR

SERVES 4

V- PK+

INGREDIENTS

1.5	WHITE ONIONS
3 THUMBS	GRATED GINGER
4-6	SMALL HOT CHILLIS
1 HANDFUL	SUNFLOWER SEEDS
4 MEDIUM	CARROTS
1 RED	BELL PEPPER
1 GREEN	BELL PEPPER
550 g	DRY BOILED LONG GRAIN BROWN RICE
1	LIME (JUICE)
4	SPRING ONIONS

2 TBSP	COCONUT OIL
0.5 TSP	SICHUAN PEPPERCORNS (GROUND)
1.5 TSP	MUSTARD SEEDS
1 TSP	BLACK PEPPER
500ML	FILTERED WATER
3 TBSP	AGAVE NECTAR
0.45 TSP	HIMALAYAN SALT
2 TSP	CORIANDER SEEDS (GROUND)

METHOD

1. PUT THE RICE ON TO BOIL, TIMING IT FOR AROUND 30 MINUTES, CHECKING AND STIRRING OCCASIONALLY.
2. THINLY SLICE THE WHITE ONION, HEAT THE COCONUT OIL IN A WOK ON A MEDIUM HEAT AND ADD THE SLICED WHITE ONIONS, GROUND SICHUAN PEPPERCORNS AND MUSTARD SEEDS. STIRFRY FOR 3 MINUTES, THEN ADD THE BLACK PEPPER, 300ML OF WATER AND AGAVE NECTAR. STIR FRY FOR ANOTHER 2 MINUTES.
3. ADD THE GRATED GINGER, CHOPPED CHILLIS, SUNFLOWER SEEDS AND SALT AND COOK FOR 2 MORE MINUTES, ENSURING THE MIX DOES NOT BURN OR STICK TO THE WOK.
4. DICE THE CARROTS INTO 1CM PIECES AND ADD THEM TO COOK FOR ANOTHER 3 MINUTES, COVERING THE WOK AND STIRRING OCCASIONALLY. ADD THE REMAINING WATER IF THE MIX IS DRY.
5. TURN THE HEAT TO LOW-MEDIUM. DICE AND ADD THE RED AND GREEN PEPPERS TO COOK FOR 2 MORE MINUTES.
6. ADD THE BOILED RICE TO THE WOK AND STIR IT IN WELL, MAKING SURE IT DOES NOT STICK TO THE WOK AND COOK FOR ANOTHER 2 MINUTES.
7. TURN OFF THE HEAT, SQUEEZE THE LIME OVER THE MIXTURE AND ADD THE FRESHLY GROUND CORIANDER SEEDS AND SPRING ONION. MIX WELL AND LET STAND FOR ANOTHER 5 MINUTES FOR THE FLAVOURS TO INFUSE.

SERVE AND ENJOY!

A CLASSIC AYURVEDIC DISH FOR RE-BUILDING THE BODY AND NOURISHING THE TISSUES.
IT IS PARTICULARLY GREAT FOR VATAS AND CAN BE TAKEN DURING OR AFTER ILLNESS.

ONE-POT KITCHARI

INGREDIENTS

50g MUNG BEANS
130g BROWN LONG-GRAIN RICE
700ML FILTERED WATER
0.25 TSP HIMALAYAN SALT
0.25 TSP GROUND TUMERIC
0.25 TSP GROUND CUMIN
0.25 TSP GROUND GINGER
0.25 TSP BLACK PEPPER
2 PINCHES CAYENNE PEPPER
1 PINCH ASAFOETIDA
2 TBSP SESAME OIL
1 TSP SESAME SEEDS
0.5 HANDFUL FRESH CORIANDER
0.5 AVOCADO
0.25 LIME (JUICE)
100g BABY SPINACH.

40 MINUTES

SERVES 2

ALL YEAR ROUND

VP ~ K+

METHOD

1. ADD THE DRY MUNG BEANS, RICE, SALT, TUMERIC, CUMIN, GINGER, BLACK PEPPER, CAYENNE AND ASAFOETIDA TO A MEDIUM POT. BOIL THE WATER SEPARATELY AND COVER THE INGREDIENTS WITH THE WATER ONCE BOILED. THERE SHOULD BE AROUND 5CM OF WATER ABOVE THE RICE.

2. PUT THE HEAT ON A MEDIUM-HIGH HEAT, AND BRING THE RICE MIXTURE TO BOIL UNTIL THERE IS NO MORE WATER AND THE RICE IS COOKED. THIS SHOULD TAKE AROUND 25 MINUTES. STIR OCCASIONALLY THROUGHOUT TO AVOID STICKING TO THE PAN. TURN OFF THE HEAT ONCE COOKED.

3. SLICE THE AVOCADO INTO SMALL CUBES AND CHOP THE FRESH CORIANDER BEFORE ADDING THEM TO THE POT, ALONG WITH THE LIME JUICE, BABY SPINACH AND SESAME OIL. STIR THE MIXTURE UNTIL THE SPINACH SOFTENS.

4. SERVE WITH A SPRINKLE OF SESAME SEEDS AND ENJOY!

GF
V
S
SPROUTED
PLANT
CHILLI
INGREDIENTS
3 THUMBS GRATED GINGER
1 MEDIUM LEEK
1 FENNEL HEAD
2 LARGE PLUM TOMATOES
3 HOT RED CHILLIS
4 STICKS CELERY
1 SMALL GREEN BELL PEPPER
1 SMALL ZUCCHINI
1 LONG RED BELL PEPPER
1 LIME (JUICE)
1 HANDFUL FRESH PARSLEY
0.5 HANDFUL FRESH CORIANDER
200g SPROUTED CHICKPEAS
200g SPROUTED ADZUKI BEANS
3 TBSP OLIVE OIL
1 CAN ORGANIC CHOPPED TOMATOES
300ML FILTERED WATER
1.5 TSP CUMIN SEEDS
1.5 TSP CAYENNE PEPPER
1.5 TSP PAPRIKA
1.5 TSP HOT CHILLI POWDER
1 TSP CHILLI FLAKES
1 TSP HIMALAYAN SALT
1 TSP BLACK PEPPER
1.5 TSP CORIANDER SEEDS

SERVES 4 1 HOUR P+ UK- AUTUMN, WINTER SPRING

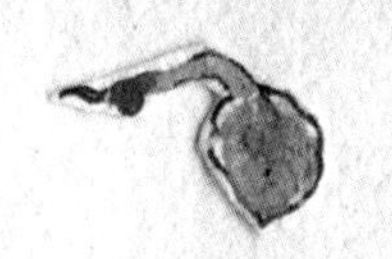

METHOD

1. USE OUR 'SPROUTED (ALMOST) ANYTHING' RECIPE TO SPROUT THE CHICKPEAS AND ADZUKI BEANS BEFORE BEGINNING. ALTERNATIVELY, YOU CAN SOAK THEM FOR 2 HOURS AND PRE-COOKING FOR 30 MINUTES OR UNTIL SOFT.

2. CHOP THE LEEK AND FENNEL HEAD INTO 1.5CM PIECES. PEEL AND GRATE THE GINGER. HEAT THE OLIVE OIL ON A LOW-MEDIUM HEAT IN A DEEP POT. ADD THESE INGREDIENTS TO THE POT AND STIR FOR 5 MINUTES.

3. ADD THE CUMIN SEEDS, CAYENNE PEPPER, PAPRIKA, HOT CHILLI POWDER, CHILLI FLAKES, SALT AND BLACK PEPPER TO THE POT, STIRRING THEM INTO THE MIX FOR 2 MINUTES.

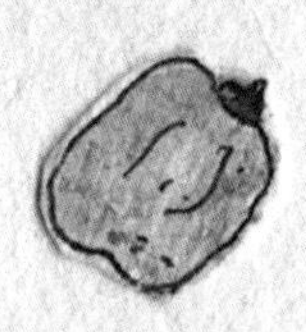

4. CHOP THE PLUM TOMATOES INTO CHUNKS, FINELY DICE THE CHILLIS AND CHOP THE CELERY INTO 1CM PIECES. ADD THESE INGREDIENTS ALONG WITH A CAN OF CHOPPED TOMATOES AND THE WATER TO THE POT. STIR TOGETHER AND BRING TO SIMMER FOR 12 MINUTES.

5. CHOP THE GREEN PEPPER INTO 2CM CHUNKS, CHOP THE ZUCCHINI AND LONG RED PEPPER IN HALF, WIDTH-WAYS, AND THEN INTO 1CM STRIPS. ADD THESE TO THE POT WITH HALF-A-LIME'S JUICE. MIX THE INGREDIENTS TOGETHER AND SIMMER FOR A FURTHER 12 MINUTES.

6. ADD THE SOAKED OR SPROUTED CHICKPEAS AND ADZUKI BEANS TO COOK FOR 10 MINUTES.

7. USING A PESTLE AND MORTAR, GRIND THE CORIANDER SEEDS, CHOP THE FRESH PARSLEY AND CORIANDER TO FINALLY ADD THESE LAST INGREDIENTS TO THE POT. TURN OFF THE HEAT AND ALLOW THE CHILLI TO STAND FOR 15 MINUTES, BEFORE TAKING A TASTY BITE – YUM!

THYME
THYME HAS ANTISEPTIC PROPERTIES THAT HAVE A SOOTHING EFFECT ON A SORE THROAT, SO IT IS QUITE A MAGICAL HERB.

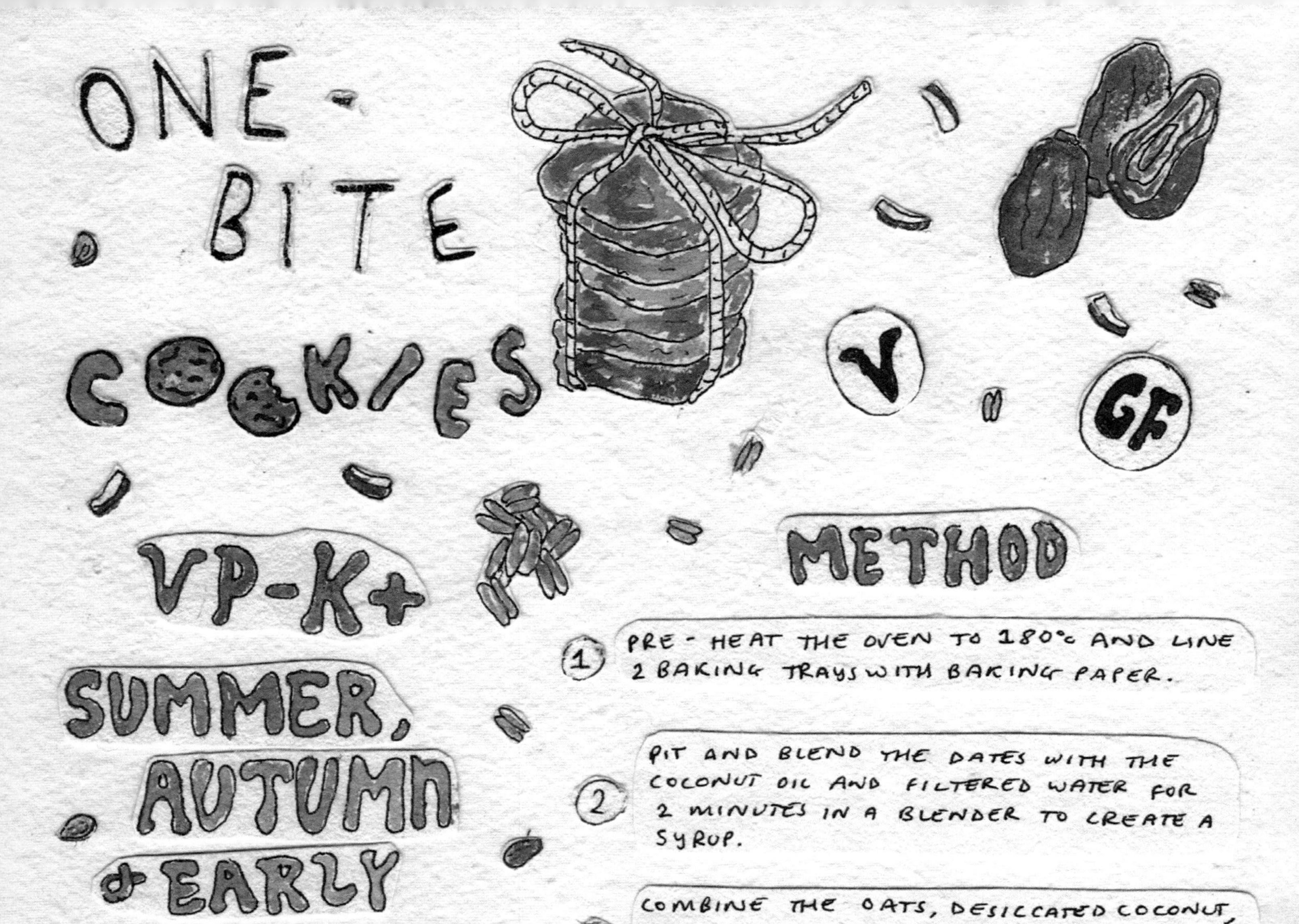

ONE-BITE COOKIES

V GF

VP-K+

SUMMER, AUTUMN & EARLY WINTER

INGREDIENTS

10	MEDJOOL DATES
200ML	FILTERED WATER
4 TBSP	ORGANIC COCONUT OIL
250g	GLUTEN FREE OATS
70g	DESICCATED COCONUT
30g	RAISINS
40g	CRUSHED WALNUTS
30g	SUNFLOWER SEEDS
1 TSP	MIXED SPICE
1.5 TSP	CINNAMON
4 TBSP	CRUNCHY PEANUT BUTTER

METHOD

1. PRE-HEAT THE OVEN TO 180°C AND LINE 2 BAKING TRAYS WITH BAKING PAPER.
2. PIT AND BLEND THE DATES WITH THE COCONUT OIL AND FILTERED WATER FOR 2 MINUTES IN A BLENDER TO CREATE A SYRUP.
3. COMBINE THE OATS, DESICCATED COCONUT, RAISINS, WALNUTS, SUNFLOWER SEEDS, MIXED SPICE AND CINNAMON IN A LARGE MIXING BOWL AND MIX TOGETHER WELL.
4. ADD THE DATE SYRUP TO THE MIXING BOWL AND USE YOUR CLEAN HANDS TO MASSAGE THE MIX THOROUGHLY TOGETHER.
5. USING YOUR HANDS, MOULD THE MIXTURE INTO INDIVIDUAL GOLF BALL SIZED BALLS, THEN USING THE PALMS OF YOUR HANDS TO FLATTEN THEM TO A THICKNESS OF 1.5cm. PLACE THEM ONTO THE TRAYS.
6. PLACE THE TRAYS INTO THE OVEN FOR 18-21 MINUTES, OR UNTIL THE COOKIES ARE A LIGHT-MEDIUM GLAZED BROWN. LEAVE THEM TO STAND FOR 10 MINUTES BEFORE TAKING A SWEET BITE AND GOING TO COOKIE HEAVEN...

ON SOMEONE'S SPECIAL DAY.

VPK+ (IN EXCESS)

SERVES 8-10

2 HOURS

V

BASE INGREDIENTS

- 200g WALNUTS
- 70g GROUND ALMONDS OR RAW ALMONDS
- 220g GRATED CARROTS
- 280g GRATED BEETROOT
- 80g GRATED GINGER ROOT
- 380g PITTED MEDJOOL DATES
- 4 TBSP GROUND FLAXSEED
- 2 TSP CINNAMON POWDER

* SOAK THE CASHEWS IN WARM WATER FOR 30 MINUTES FOR THE FROSTING *

1. ADD THE WALNUTS, AND THE ALMONDS IF YOU AREN'T USING GROUND ALMONDS, TO A FOOD PROCESSOR OR BLENDER AND PROCESS THE NUTS FOR 1-2 MINUTES UNTIL THE NUTS RESEMBLE A THICK POWDER. IF YOU ARE USING A BLENDER YOU MAY NEED TO GIVE THE MIX A STIR OCCASIONALLY IF THE MIX BECOMES STUCK. ADD THIS POWDER INTO A MIXING BOWL WITH THE GROUND ALMONDS (IF USING).
2. PEEL AND FINELY GRATE THE CARROTS, BEETROOT AND GINGER. ADD THESE TO THE BLENDER OR FOOD PROCESSOR AND PROCESS FOR 1 MINUTE. THE MIXTURE SHOULD BE CHUNKY AND <u>NOT</u> PASTE-LIKE. AGAIN, STIR, IF NEEDED. POP THESE INTO THE MIXING BOWL.
3. PIT AND FINELY CHOP THE DATES UNTIL THEY RESEMBLE A DENSE PASTE. ADD THESE TO THE MIXING BOWL ALONG WITH THE GROUND FLAXSEED AND CINNAMON POWDER.
4. PREPARE A SPRINGFORM PAN (WE USE A 20CM DIAMETER x 4.5CM DEPTH PAN). USE YOUR CLEAN HANDS TO MASSAGE THE MIXTURE TOGETHER FOR AROUND 2-3 MINUTES, MAKING SURE THE INGREDIENTS ARE WELL COMBINED.
5. POP THE MIX INTO THE SPRINGFORM PAN AND USE THE BOTTOM OF A GLASS TO PRESS IT DOWN EVENLY AND FIRMLY TO FLATTEN THE BASE. LEAVE 1.5-2CM OF SPACE FOR THE FROSTING ON TOP OF THE BASE.

TURN ME OVER FOR THE FROSTING! →

FROSTING METHOD

FROSTING INGREDIENTS

250g	RAW CASHENS
100g	MATURE COCONUT FLESH
0.5 CANS	ORGANIC COCONUT MILK
0.25	LEMON (JUICE)
50ML	FILTERED WATER
0.25	POMEGRANATE (SEEDS)
0.25 TSP	CINNAMON POWDER

1. CAREFULLY REMOVE THE COCONUT FLESH FROM THE SHELL AND CUT IT INTO 2CM CHUNKS. IN A BLENDER OR A FOOD PROCESSOR, DRAIN AND COMBINE THE SOAKED CASHEWS, COCONUT CHUNKS, COCONUT MILK, LEMON JUICE AND WATER. PROCESS FOR 2-3 MINUTES, UNTIL IT IS SMOOTH WITHOUT LUMPS.
2. POUR THE MIX EVENLY OVER THE BASE IN THE SPRINGFORM TIN. USE A SPOON OR SPATULA TO EVENLY SPREAD OUT THE FROSTING.
3. REMOVE THE POMEGRANATE SEEDS FROM THE FRUIT AND SPRINKLE THEM OVER THE FROSTING. LIGHTLY DUST THE CINNAMON OVER THE TOP.
4. COVER AND POP THE CAKE IN THE FREEZER OVERNIGHT. REMOVE FROM THE FREEZER AROUND 4 HOURS BEFORE SERVING TO ALLOW IT TO THAW PROPERLY!

CASHEW NUTS ARE FAIRLY HEAVY AND GROUNDING IN NATURE SO THEY CAN HELP TO STABILISE THE NERVOUS-SYSTEM, ESPECIALLY IN AUTUMN, WHEN VATA (NERVOUSNESS) TENDS TO BE AGGRAVATED!

FYI!

CASHEWS ALSO BUILD TISSUE, STRENGTH AND STAMINA BUT BE AWARE THAT THEY ARE 'RAJASIC' IN NATURE (STIMULATES MOVEMENT) SO IT IS BEST TO SNACK ON SOMETHING ELSE IF ONE INTENDS TO BE STILL OR RESTED.

INGREDIENTS

RICE

350g BROWN RICE
1L FILTERED WATER
75g MATURE COCONUT FLESH
OR 1 YOUNG COCONUT FLESH
1 CAN ORGANIC COCONUT MILK
1-2 TBSP FRESH HONEY OR AGAVE NECTAR (IF VEGAN)

SAUCE

2 LARGE MANGOES
1 TSP LEMON (JUICE)

SERVES 4-5

1 HOUR
(+1 HOUR SETTING-TIME)

METHOD

1. COVER THE RICE WITH WATER AND SOAK FOR 30 MINUTES. STRAIN AND ADD THE RICE TO A MEDIUM POT. BOIL 1L OF WATER SEPARATELY, THEN USE IT TO COVER THE RICE. (THE WATER SHOULD BE 5CM ABOVE THE RICE LEVEL).

2. BRING THE POT TO BOIL ON A MEDIUM-HIGH HEAT. COOK THE RICE FOR 20 MINUTES, OR UNTIL THE WATER IS COMPLETELY ABSORBED AND THE RICE IS SOFT. STIR OCCASIONALLY TO ENSURE THE RICE DOESN'T STICK TO THE POT.

3. WHILST THE RICE IS COOKING, CAREFULLY CHOP THE MATURE COCONUT FLESH, OR SCOOP OUT THE YOUNG COCONUT AND ADD THIS TO A BLENDER, ALONG WITH THE COCONUT MILK AND HONEY/AGAVE NECTAR. BLEND FOR 2 MINUTES UNTIL SMOOTH.

4. WHEN THE RICE IS COOKED, TURN OFF THE HEAT AND POUR THE BLENDED MIX OVER THE RICE, STIRRING TO COAT THE RICE WELL. SET THIS MIXTURE INTO A RECTANGULAR DISH (WE USED A 24CM × 16CM BAKING DISH). USE A LARGE SPOON TO TIGHTLY PRESS THE RICE TO THE BOTTOM OF THE DISH. LEAVE TO STAND AT ROOM TEMPERATURE FOR AT LEAST 1 HOUR.

5. TO MAKE THE SAUCE, ADD THE FLESH OF 1 MANGO, WITH THE LEMON JUICE TO A BLENDER AND BLEND FOR 1 MINUTE, UNTIL SMOOTH. ADD TO A POURING JUG FOR SERVING. PEEL AND SLICE THE REMAINING MANGO TO YOUR LIKING.

6. TO SERVE, SCOOP THE RICE INTO BOWLS, POURING THE SAUCE OVER THE RICE AND GARNISHING WITH THE FRESH CUT MANGO!

FYI!

THESE BITES ARE FOR THE LOVERS... NATURALLY APHRODISIACS, DATES IMPROVE SPERM QUANTITY AND QUALITY IN MEN.

A LITTLE NOTE OF CAUTION – AS THESE BALLS ARE FULL PACKED WITH ENERGY WE RECOMMEND ONLY EATING THEM IF YOU PLAN TO BE ACTIVE, IF YOU GET WHAT WE MEAN :)

'ON A DATE' ENERGY BARS

MAKES ~ 30-40 BITES

ALL YEAR ROUND

20 MINUTES (+2 HOURS)

VPK ~

K V R GF

INGREDIENTS

- 400g PITTED MEDJOOL DATES
- 100g GRATED GINGER
- 100g CHIA SEEDS
- 100g GLUTEN-FREE OATS
- 200ml FILTERED WATER
- 50g HEMP SEEDS
- 50g CACAO POWDER
- 1.5 TSP CRUSHED CHILLIS
- 1 TSP CINNAMON
- 0.25 TSP HIMALAYAN SALT

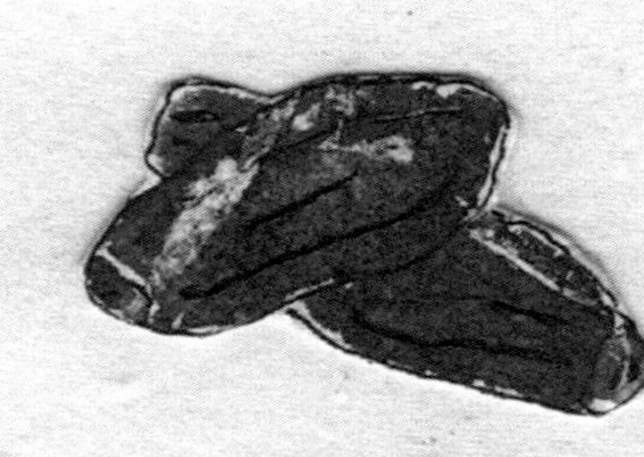

METHOD

1. PIT AND CHOP THE DATES USING A LARGE KNIFE UNTIL THEY RESEMBLE A LARGE PULP. PEEL AND GRATE THE GINGER AND ADD THESE INGREDIENTS ALONG WITH THE CHIA SEEDS, OATS, WATER, HEMP SEEDS, CACAO POWDER, CRUSHED CHILLIS, CINNAMON AND SALT TO A MIXING BOWL.
2. USE YOUR CLEAN HANDS TO MASSAGE THE INGREDIENTS TOGETHER; MAKE SURE TO MIX THE MIXTURE WELL TOGETHER INTO A HOMOGENOUS MASS.
3. LINE A RECTANGULAR VESSEL (WE USE A 24CM+16CM BAKING DISH) WITH BAKING PAPER AND SCOOP THE MIXTURE INTO THE DISH. USE THE BOTTOM OF A GLASS TO PRESS THE MIX FIRMLY TO EVENLY COVER THE BOTTOM OF THE DISH.
4. REFRIGERATE FOR AT LEAST 2 HOURS AND THEN CUT INTO SMALL 3CM x 1CM BITES. REFRIGERATE THE BITES FOR UP TO 4 WEEKS AND ENJOY WHEN NEEDED :)!

FYI!

OUR TWIST ON THE CLASSIC BANANA BREAD.
VERY EASY TO MAKE AND EVEN EASIER TO EAT!

HAVE ME AS A SNACK OR DESERT

CACAO NIBS ARE PACKED WITH ANTIOXIDANTS, BUT, JUST LIKE ANY OTHER CHOCOLATE, SHOULD BE ENJOYED IN MODERATION AS IT CAN AGGRAVATE VATA AND PITTA IN EXCESS.

Babanana Bites

VPwK+ (in excess)

Makes 16 balls

Summer, autumn, early winter

10 minutes

Eat me within 2-3 days!

Method

1. Pop the oats and cinnamon in a dry blender or food processor. Blend for 30 seconds until the mix resembles a powder. Pour the mix into a mixing bowl.

2. Use the back of a knife to crush the walnuts and then chop them finely. Add these, along with 20g of cacao nibs to the mixing bowl.

3. Pit and chop the dates finely. Peel and break up the bananas into small pieces and add these and the dates to the blender or food processor. Pulse for 2 minutes or until the mix resembles a thick paste. If you are using a blender, you may need to give it a stir to avoid sticking. Add this mix to the mixing bowl.

4. Use a wooden spoon to stir the mixture together for a couple of minutes until the ingredients are well-combined and thick.

5. Scatter the remaining cacao nibs on a plate. Wet your hands slightly (to prevent sticking) and begin to form the mix into golf-sized balls. Roll them gently in the cacao nibs before placing them on another plate.

6. When complete, refrigerate for 2+ hours or enjoy freshly rolled.

Ingredients

- 200g gluten free rolled oats
- 1.5tsp ground cinnamon
- 60g walnuts
- 70g cacao nibs
- 3 bananas (very ripe)
- 5-8 medjool dates

Sips
TEJAS
GOLDEN MYLK
LIQUORICE & GINGER TEA
ROSE & FENNEL TEA
THE OJAS
HIBISCUS

TEJAS
A SANSKRIT NAME MEANING POWER, BRILLIANCE, ENERGY OR A NAME FOR THE ELEMENT OF FIRE.
IF YOU LIVE IN THE TROPICS AND HAVE EVEN A SMALL BIT OF SOIL TO GROW PLANTS, THEN MAKE A SPECIAL PLACE TO GROW TUMERIC AND GINGER ROOT.
THEY GROW BEAUTIFUL FLOWERS...
AND THEY DON'T NEED TOO MUCH DEPTH OR EFFORT...
TO FLOURISH!
PLUS... THEY TASTE AMAZING!

AUTUMN, WINTER, SPRING.

5 MINUTES

VK-P+

1 MUG

TEJAS

INGREDIENTS

0.25 TSP	TUMERIC POWDER
1 TSP	FRESH GINGER
1 PINCH	CAYENNE PEPPER
1 PINCH	BLACK PEPPER
300ML	FILTERED WATER

METHOD

1. BOIL THE WATER AND PEEL AND GRATE THE GINGER.
2. ADD ALL THE INGREDIENTS WITH THE BOILING WATER INTO YOUR FAVOURITE MUG! GIVE IT A STIR TO MIX THE TEA TOGETHER.

* YOU MAY WISH TO REFIL YOUR MUG WITH HOT WATER FOR ROUND 2 AS THE SPICES TEND TO SETTLE AT THE BOTTOM OF THE MUG.

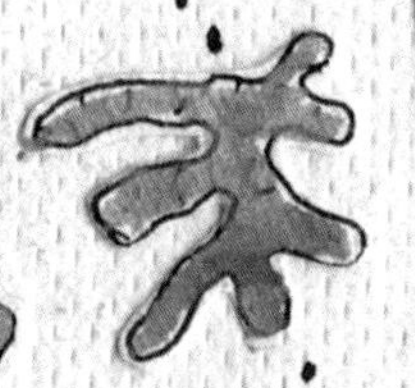

VPK~

ALL YEAR ROUND

1 MUG

10 MINUTES

Golden MYLK

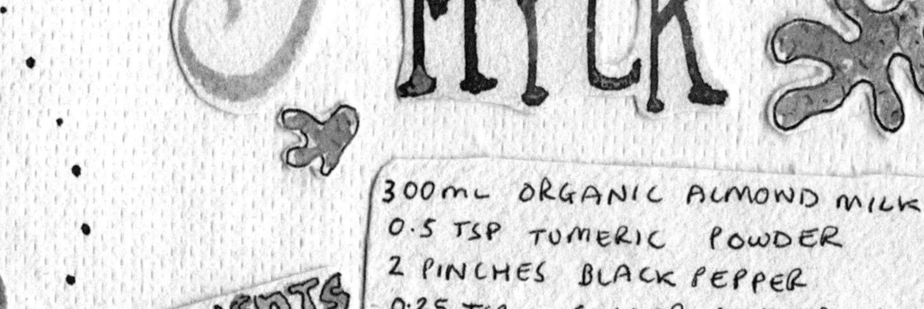

INGREDIENTS

300ML	ORGANIC ALMOND MILK
0.5 TSP	TUMERIC POWDER
2 PINCHES	BLACK PEPPER
0.25 TSP	GINGER POWDER
0.25 TSP	ASHWAGANDHA
0.5 TSP	CINNAMON
1 TSP	AGAVE NECTAR (OPTIONAL)

METHOD

1. IN A POT, ON A LOW-MEDIUM HEAT, COMBINE THE INGREDIENTS TOGETHER AND STIR WELL FOR AROUND 10 MINUTES.
2. WHEN THE MYLK BEGINS TO BOIL, TURN OFF THE HEAT AND USING A HAND BLENDER, BLEND THE MIXTURE CAREFULLY. MAKE SURE IT DOESN'T SPLASH EVERYWHERE AND GIVE YOUR KITCHEN YELLOW POLKA-DOTS!
3. POUR INTO YOUR FAVOURITE MUG AND ENJOY (PARTICULARLY IN THE MORNING OR LATE EVENING!)

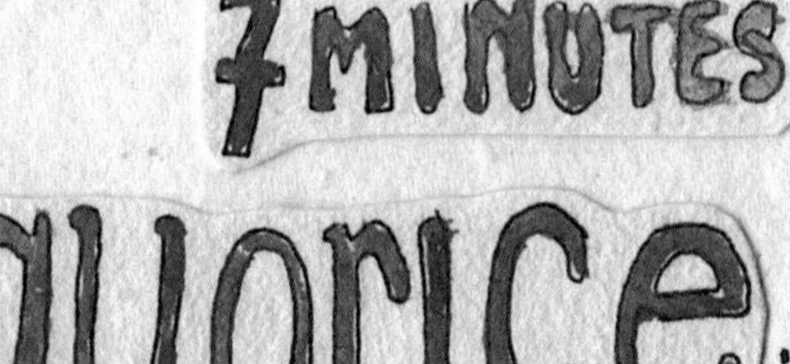

Liquorice and Ginger

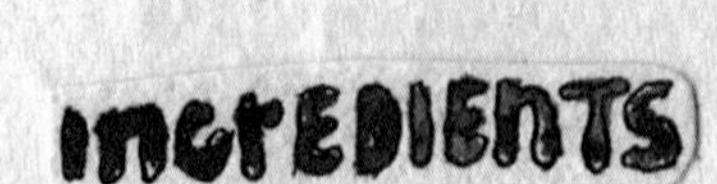

0.25 TSP LIQUORICE POWDER
0.25 TSP GINGER POWDER
300ML FILTERED WATER

METHOD

1. BOIL THE WATER AND POUR THIS OVER THE LIQUORICE AND GINGER POWDER IN YOUR PREFERRED CUP. STIR TOGETHER AND ALLOW TO STEEP FOR 3 MINUTES BEFORE ENJOYING!

* THE INGREDIENTS TEND TO SINK SO TOP UP WITH HOT WATER, STIR AND ENJOY ANOTHER CUPPA!

ALL YEAR ROUND 1 MUG
7 MINUTES VPK~

Rose and Fennel

INGREDIENTS

1 TSP ROSE PETALS
0.5 TSP FENNEL SEEDS
300ML FILTERED WATER

METHOD

1. BOIL THE WATER AND ADD THIS, ALONG WITH THE ROSE PETALS AND FENNEL SEEDS TO YOUR COSIEST MUG. STIR AND ALLOW TO STEEP FOR 3 MINUTES BEFORE ENJOYING.

* TOP UP WITH HOT WATER FOR ROUND 2.

ROSE HELPS TO SOOTHE THE HEART AND EMOTIONS.
IT IS COOLING, YET IT STRENGTHENS AGNI (DIGESTIVE FIRE), MAKING IT PERFECT FOR ANYONE TO ENJOY!
FYI!
LIQUORICE HAS 50X THE NATURAL SWEETNESS OF REFINED SUGAR!
IT IS A STRONG ADRENAL TONIC, PROVIDING STRENGTH TO THE WHOLE BODY AND NOURISHMENT TO THE NERVOUS SYSTEM!

FYI!
HIBISCUS FLOWER IS COOLING
AND A DIURETIC FOR THE BODY.
IT IMPROVES LIVER FUNCTION
AND ALLEVIATES CONSTIPATION!
SUNFLOWER SEEDS HELP TO
REDUCE INFLAMMATION,
REGULATE CHOLESTEROL
AND DETOXIFY THE
BODY!
TRY ADDING
THEM
SPROUTED
FYI!

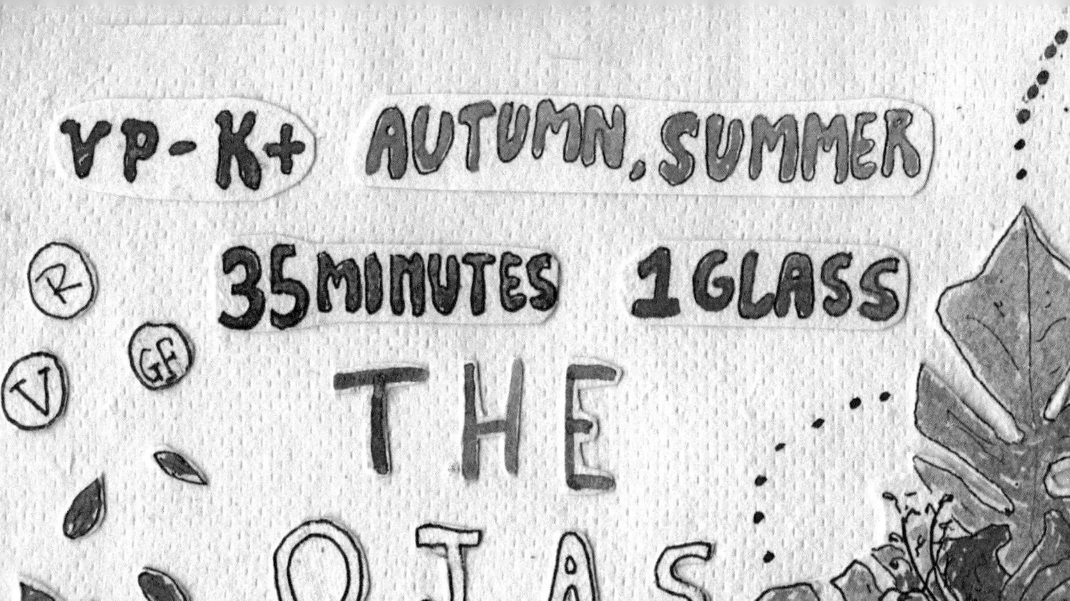

VP-K+ AUTUMN, SUMMER

35 MINUTES 1 GLASS

(R) (V) (GF)

THE OJAS

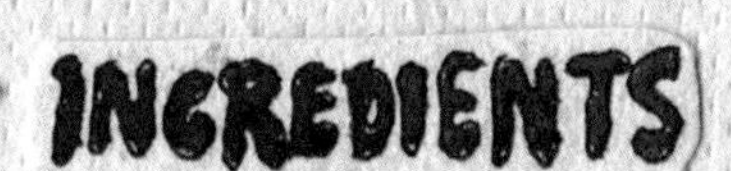

INGREDIENTS

1 HANDFUL	RAW ALMONDS
OR	SUNFLOWER SEEDS
0·5 TSP	FENNEL SEEDS
300 ML	FILTERED WATER
3	DATES

METHOD

1. PIT THE DATES
2. COMBINE ALL INGREDIENTS INTO A BLENDER AND BLEND FOR AROUND 2 MINUTES AND THE SMOOTHIE IS SMOOOOTH.
3. POUR AND SERVE!

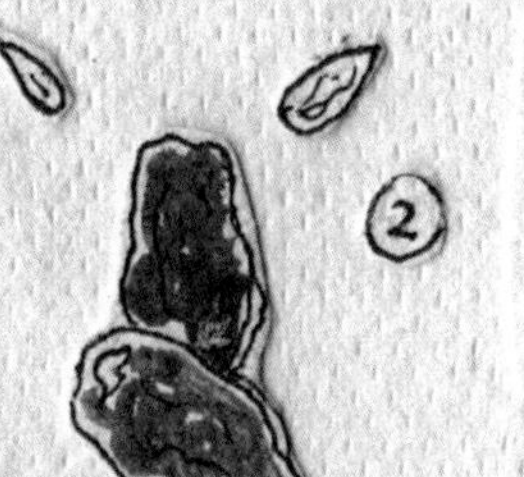

ALL YEAR ROUND VPK~

5 MINUTES 1 GLASS

(V) (GF) (Vg)

HIBISCUS

INGREDIENTS

9 DRIED	HIBISCUS HEADS
3 TSP	HONEY / AGAVE NECTAR
900 ML	FILTERED WATER.

METHOD

1. BOIL THE WATER AND POUR THIS OVER THE DRIED HIBISCUS IN A JUG.
2. LEAVE TO COOL AND INFUSE FOR 30 MINUTES.
3. REMOVE THE HIBISCUS AND ADD THE HONEY OR AGAVE NECTAR, STIRRING TO DISOLVE IT.
4. ENJOY WARM!

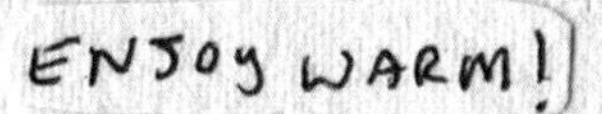

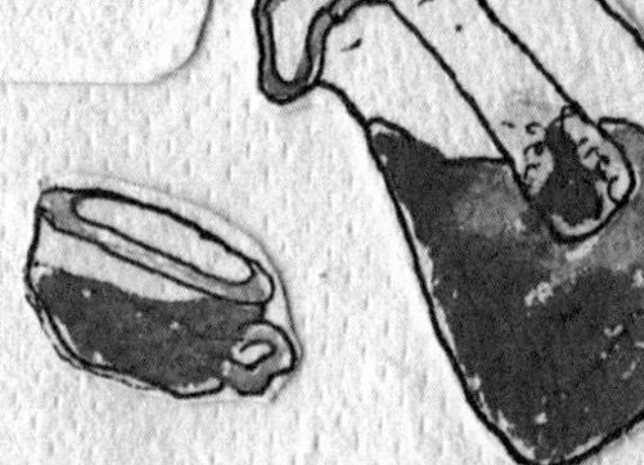

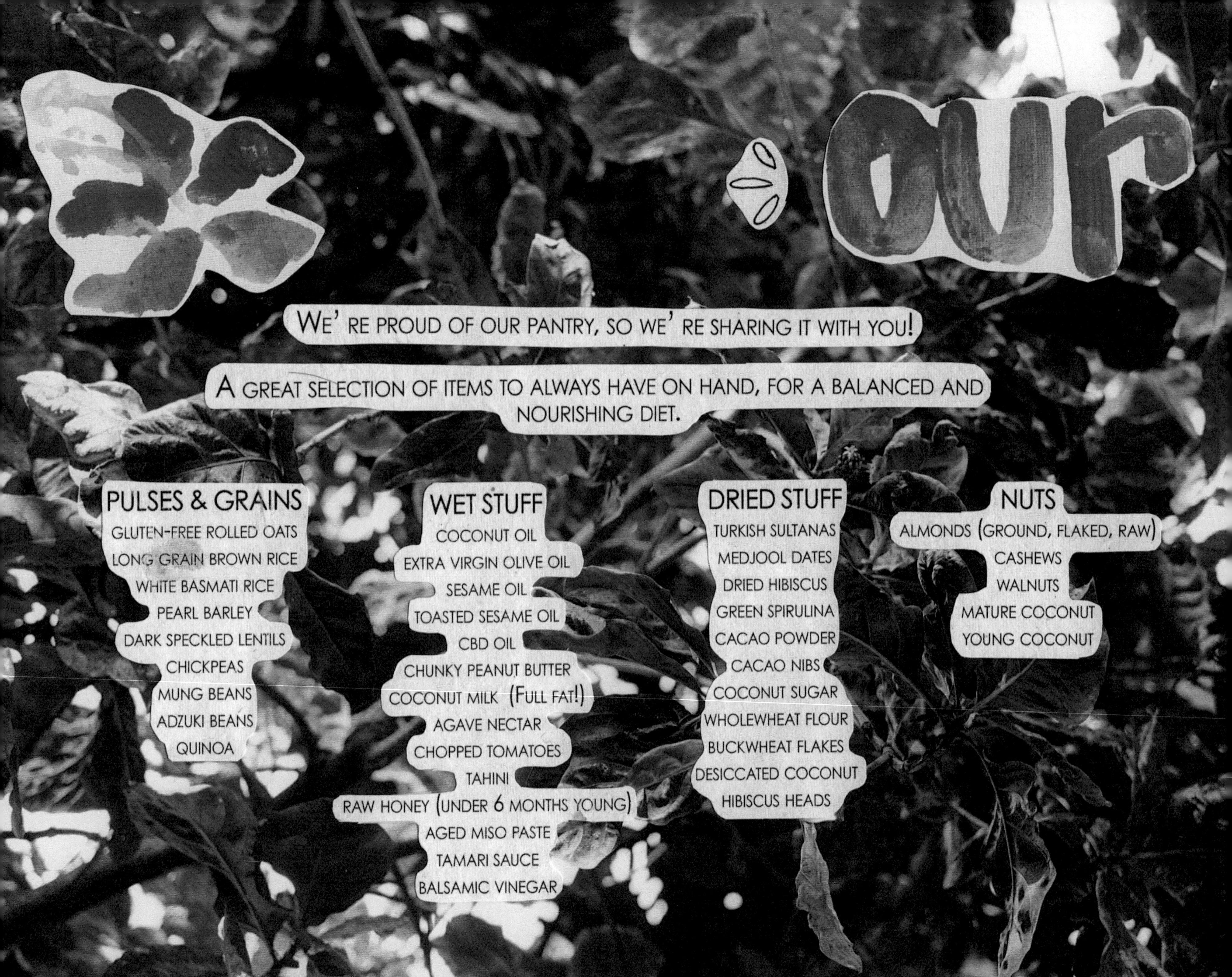
our
We' re proud of our pantry, so we' re sharing it with you!
A great selection of items to always have on hand, for a balanced and nourishing diet.
PULSES & GRAINS
GLUTEN-FREE ROLLED OATS
LONG GRAIN BROWN RICE
WHITE BASMATI RICE
PEARL BARLEY
DARK SPECKLED LENTILS
CHICKPEAS
MUNG BEANS
ADZUKI BEANS
QUINOA
WET STUFF
COCONUT OIL
EXTRA VIRGIN OLIVE OIL
SESAME OIL
TOASTED SESAME OIL
CBD OIL
CHUNKY PEANUT BUTTER
COCONUT MILK (FULL FAT!)
AGAVE NECTAR
CHOPPED TOMATOES
TAHINI
RAW HONEY (UNDER 6 MONTHS YOUNG)
AGED MISO PASTE
TAMARI SAUCE
BALSAMIC VINEGAR
DRIED STUFF
TURKISH SULTANAS
MEDJOOL DATES
DRIED HIBISCUS
GREEN SPIRULINA
CACAO POWDER
CACAO NIBS
COCONUT SUGAR
WHOLEWHEAT FLOUR
BUCKWHEAT FLAKES
DESICCATED COCONUT
HIBISCUS HEADS
NUTS
ALMONDS (GROUND, FLAKED, RAW)
CASHEWS
WALNUTS
MATURE COCONUT
YOUNG COCONUT

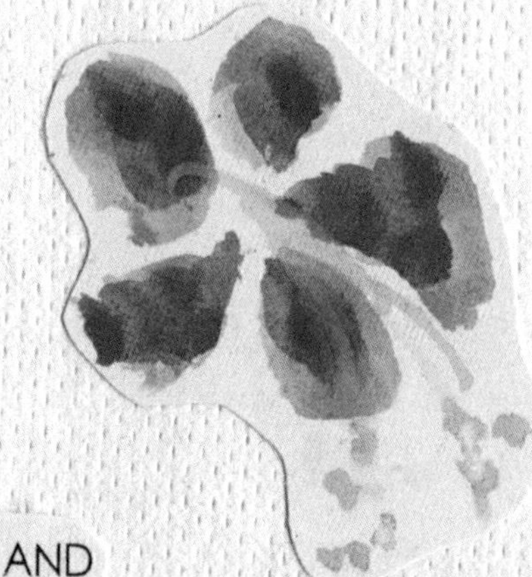

We highly recommend that all of these base-products be Organic and from a reputable source.

Buying non-organic products like these risks nasty additives and preservatives sneaking their way into your diet.

ROOTS

- GALANGAL
- TURMERIC
- GINGER

SEEDS

- CARDAMOM PODS
- CARAWAY SEEDS
- NIGELLA SEEDS
- MUSTARD SEEDS
- FENUGREEK SEEDS
- CORIANDER SEEDS
- CUMIN SEEDS
- SESAME SEEDS
- SUNFLOWER SEEDS
- PUMPKIN SEEDS
- GROUND FLAXSEED
- CHIA SEEDS
- FENNEL SEEDS

DRY HERBS & SPICES

- ASHWAGANDHA
- AJWAN
- GROUND GINGER
- PAPRIKA (SMOKED AND NORMAL)
- CHILLI FLAKES
- TURMERIC POWDER
- PINK HIMALAYAN SALT
- BLACK PEPPER
- GARAM MASALA
- GINGER POWDER
- CAYENNE PEPPER
- CORIANDER POWDER
- GROUND CINNAMON
- BAY LEAVES
- CURRY LEAVES
- SICHUAN PEPPERCORNS
- CLOVES

LIVING HERBS

- BASIL
- ROSEMARY
- OREGANO
- PARSLEY
- THYME
- CORIANDER
- LEMONGRASS

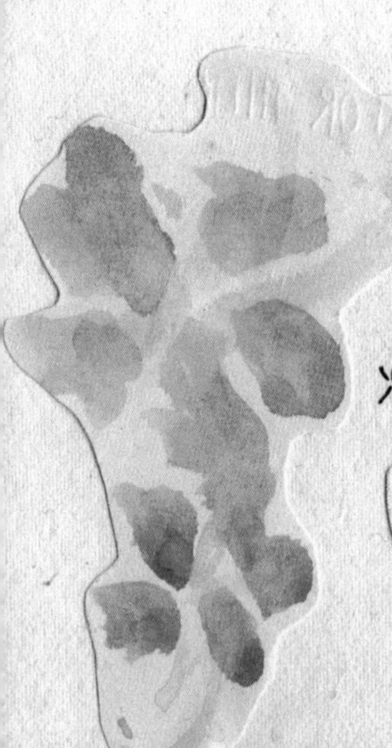

THANK YOU FOR JOINING OUR JOURNEY!

OUR BLESSINGS ARE WITH YOU ON YOUR UNIQUE PATH,
WHEREVER YOU HAVE COME FROM AND
WHEREVER YOU MAY GO.

··NAMASTE··

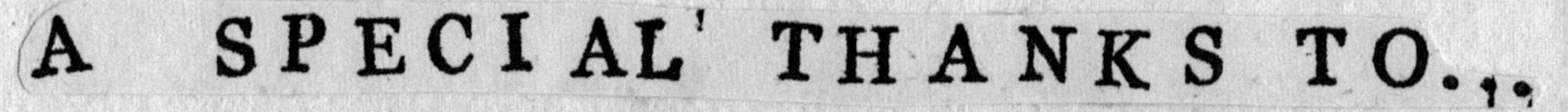

OUR DEAR FAMILY AND FRIENDS FOR THEIR
GUIDANCE, SUPPORT AND UNDIVIDED LOVE.

A CIP catalogue record for this title is available from the British Library.

ISBN 9781398484993 (Paperback)
ISBN 9781398485006 (Hardback)
ISBN 9781398485013 (ePub e-book)

www.austinmacauley.com

First Published 2022
Austin Macauley Publishers Ltd ®
1 Canada Square
Canary Wharf
London
E14 5AA